Ben Boland has a real hea
dementia and a genuine love
brings both together in a way
has the potential to help us (
fully and more faithfully in the time of dementia. This is
a lovely contribution to an important area of human life.

JOHN SWINTON
Professor in Practical Theology and Pastoral Care,
University of Aberdeen, Aberdeen

Ben has written a valuable, accessible and practical
book on ageing, dementia and pastoral care. It will be
of immense help to those who work closely with older
people, especially those beginning their pastoral and
voluntary ministry. At the same time, I am sure that
people with longer experience of ministry in these fields
will also enjoy dipping into the pages of this small book,
and will find many gems and affirmations of the work
they do. It is a book that is thoroughly Jesus focused, as it
honours the recipient of care and the caregiver.

ELIZABETH MACKINLAY
Director, Centre for Ageing and Pastoral Studies

With a key focus on praying with and for older people as
well as spending time with them, in this book Ben Boland
acknowledges that without relationship, good pastoral
care is impossible. In *Priceless People*, Boland uses his
experience as a chaplain to show how we can honour and
respect older people whilst meeting their spiritual needs.

KAREN MARTIN
Author, *Memorable Loss*

An easy read and valuable ministry resource, which benefited us and we recommend for all Christians as it combines Ben's experience, practical insights and obvious compassion for older people.

DAVID AND MAXINE COOK
Presbyterian Church of Australia

Priceless People combines theological and practical insights to challenge, prepare, and equip Christians to share Jesus' love with older people and people living with dementia. Its short length and easy readability make it accessible to those in the pews, while its depth challenges those in the pulpit. A must-read not only for those interested in ministry with older people and people living with dementia, but all Christians who want to love their neighbours.

HAROLD G. KOENIG
Director, Center for Spirituality, Theology and Health,
Duke University Medical Center, Durham, North Carolina

There are plenty of helpful practical suggestions here to help us be God's eyes and ears where older people congregate and are cared for. Anyone taking worship to older people will find much good advice in this book to shape their services, aid their listening, and join in the ways God continues to enjoy us – however frail or confused we may become – and to cherish us throughout our lives.

DEBBIE THROWER
Founder and Pioneer of Anna Chaplaincy for Older People

Do you want to know how to minister to people living with dementia, and their family and friends? Read this book! Ben has written a clear, wise, practical, theologically accurate and culturally sensitive book that I wish I had when I started ministering to older people and those living with dementia.

DAVID TYNDALL
Anglican Minister

Ben Boland has a passion for ministry with older people, and this passion shows in the pages of this book. Ben writes clearly and with warmth and enthusiasm, giving readers valuable insights into the joys and challenges of ministry to people in the later years of life. I know of no other book which addresses the issues of 'why' and 'how' Christians should engage in Christocentric ministry to people in aged care in such an engaging way. It is accessible to the novice as well as the experienced pastoral worker seeking to hone their skills in this particular pastoral context. I am sure that *Priceless People* has the potential to be a very valuable tool for use by professionals and volunteers alike engaged in pastoral care of older people and people living with dementia.

CHRISTINE BRAIN
Editor of *Mia Mia*

PRICELESS PEOPLE

Loving Older People & People & People Living with Dementia

BEN R. BOLAND

CHRISTIAN
FOCUS

In general, I have provided a reference to a chapter rather than specific verses. I believe Scripture should interpret Scripture and that context is therefore critically important.

All names have been changed to protect privacy.

Copyright © Ben R. Boland 2025

Print ISBN: 978-1-5271-1268-1
Ebook ISBN: 978-1-5271-1328-2

10 9 8 7 6 5 4 3 2 1

First published in 2025
by
Christian Focus Publications Ltd,
Geanies House, Fearn, Ross-shire,
IV20 1TW, Great Britain

www.christianfocus.com

Cover design by Rhian Muir

Printed by Bell & Bain, Glasgow

MIX
Paper | Supporting
responsible forestry
FSC
www.fsc.org
FSC® C007785

This book is dedicated to my beloved father

Robert Alfred Boland,

who taught and showed me Jesus' love both before and after he grew older and lived with more than one dementia.

Contents

Introduction

I love older people and people living with dementia, but Jesus loves them even more! That's why I became, and continue to serve as, a chaplain.

The purpose of *Priceless People* is to equip Christians to share Jesus' love more effectively with both older people and people living with dementia. This is the book I wish I'd been given when I started working as a chaplain fifteen years ago. It's not just for those in pastoral ministry. Instead, it's designed for all Christians who love, or want to love, older people. It does so by raising awareness of the importance of sharing Jesus with both older people and with people living with dementia.

Perhaps some backstory will help. *Priceless People* started life as a series of articles in *Mia Mia* (the quarterly magazine of Mother's Union Australia). The series proved helpful, so it has now grown, been reshaped, and enhanced to create this book.

Most books about ministry in the context of dementia have an early chapter defining and exploring dementia. *Priceless People* doesn't. Dementia research is constantly evolving, so any such definition risks being out of date almost immediately. There are also great websites providing information about dementia and they are regularly updated.

I need to add two important points. First, as with cancer, a person can live with more than one type of dementia. Second, though the biggest risk factor for developing dementia is growing older, dementia and ageing are not synonymous. Many older adults don't have dementia and, actually, many younger people live with it, including some children.

Thus, while sharing Jesus' love with older people and with people living with dementia constitute important topics individually, there's significant crossover in terms of principles and demographics. Much of this book's material about dementia applies to people living with it at any age.

Finally, ageing and dementia are hard and challenging topics, so I recommend reading this book slowly. Each chapter builds on the preceding chapters; however, every chapter is short and able to stand alone. So, you can either dip into specific topics, or read the book from cover to cover.

I hope and pray that this book challenges, equips and inspires you to share Jesus' love with both older people and people living with dementia.

Scripture, Growing Old and Dementia

Consider the media attention given to domestic violence (a horrific scourge).

Compare the attention given to dementia, the biggest killer of women in some high-income countries,[1] though 60 per cent of people living with dementia live in low- and middle-income countries.[2]

Contrast the attention paid to youth suicide with the scant attention afforded the most at-risk group for suicide: older men.[3]

We live in a world where the stigma of ageism is the norm,[4] a world where value is derived from economic

---

1   The biggest killer of men remains cardiovascular disease. https://www. who.int/news-room/fact-sheets/detail/the-top-10-causes-of-death

2   https://www.alzint.org/about/dementia-facts-figures/dementia-statistics/

3   The second highest suicide demographic.

4   Discrimination on the basis of age.

contribution, youth and beauty. Media representations of older people are often either openly derogatory or absent.

Indeed, a 2021 World Health Organization report found that 50 per cent of the world's population is ageist[5] and that many people living with dementia are denied basic human rights.

Christian Ageism

Consider the following test for your denomination and church: What proportion of resources (leadership, time and finances) is focused on people under twenty, versus the resources directed towards people over eighty?

In 2009, the American National Center on Elder Abuse reported that almost 50 per cent of people living with dementia experience abuse. There's also evidence that elder abuse increased during COVID-19.[6] The 2021 Australian Royal Commission into Aged Care Quality and Safety report identified that the reason aged[7] care 'has been under prolonged stress and has reached crisis point' and does 'not meet Australians' expectations', is because Australians have treated aged care as a 'lower priority' and

---

5   The World Health Organization (WHO) defines ageism as age-based stereotypes, prejudice and discrimination.

6   Weissberger, G. H., Lim, A. C., Mosqueda, L., Schoen, J., Axelrod, J., Nguyen, A. L., Wilber, K. H., Esquivel, R. S., & Han, S. D. (2022). *Elder abuse in the COVID-19 era based on calls to the National Center on Elder Abuse resource line, BMC Geriatrics*, *22*(1), 689–689. https://doi.org/10.1186/s12877-022-03385-w

7   'Aged' is now considered ageist language in much of the world however it remains the government approved language in Australia. As this book is for an international readership, I've tried to avoid referring to *aged care* except where it explicitly refers to the Australian context.

the government has responded by 'restraining aged-care expenditure' to the extent that 'funding is insufficient, insecure and subject to the fiscal priorities of the day'.

I've heard Christians say repeatedly: 'Children are the future of the church'. However, this position is unbiblical. Jesus and the early church in Acts ministered almost exclusively to adults. Yes, Christians are called to 'raise our children in ways of righteousness', yet the future of the church is conversion.

> 'Old age is not a mistake: It's actually part of God's plan for humanity.'
> —Louise Morse
> in *Dementia: Pathways to Hope; Spiritual insights and practical advice*, p. 85.

But let's start at the beginning.

Immutably valuable

Scripturally, people have at least a threefold value:

1. We're created by God.

2. We're created in God's image.

3. We're so loved by God that Jesus died for us.

Arguably the most valuable painting on earth is Da Vinci's 'Mona Lisa' (worth over US$ 860 million). Its value isn't simply the image. You can purchase a poster copy for a few dollars. The 'Mona Lisa' is valued because it was created by 'the master'. All of creation has value as it's 'God's handiwork'. Thus, creation has value beyond superficial characteristics, such as its utility or beauty, because it was made by God.

To extend the painting analogy, we're not simply painted by God, but we reflect Him. Being created by God and in His image provides the basis of our value. Therefore, our value transcends any of our characteristics such as gender, race, power, age, beauty and strength.

Any suggestion that our value was destroyed, either by the Fall or our individual sin, is quashed by Jesus. God who became human as we are human. Jesus who loved us so much, He died for us!

The basic theological point about older people and people living with dementia is that they're innately and immutably valuable and loved by God, because they, like all other people, bear the image of God.

How should Christians treat older people?

However, in addition to the immutable value of every person, the Bible clearly teaches that:

- Being old is tough (e.g. Eccles. 11).

- Christians have a particular responsibility to care for older people (e.g. Exod. 20, Eph. 6, James 1 and Matt. 25).

Historically the church has been the leader in the provision of care for older people.[8] In Australia, most aged care providers were started by churches, and many continue to be run by them.[9] My hope is that Christians and churches

---

8   John Dickson, *Bullies and Saints: An Honest Look at the Good and Evil of Christian History* (Zondervan, 2021), pp. 80-83.

9   This is also true across much of the world.

of all denominations will once again become leaders in not simply caring for older people, but in loving them wholeheartedly: physically, emotionally and spiritually.

Finding Faith in Dementia

I met Amy when she moved into a dementia-specific unit. Amy had been a teen in London during the Blitz and her dementia meant these memories were now very fresh for her. In fact, she had been moved into the secure unit because she was struggling with significant agitation, which manifested in 'behaviours' that were disturbing to others.

When I first introduced myself, Amy told me in no uncertain terms that she was not religious and had no time for God. Over time, she slowly started to engage with me and then began attending the weekly care home church service, primarily because she liked the singing. Then she started actively encouraging other residents to come too. She would repeatedly tell me 'I never had time for God but now I really like Him. I just don't know why!'

Soon after, she attended a video-based 'Introduction to Christianity' course we ran in the care home. We sat around tables and watched the video, I gave a quick summary with relevance to older people, and we had morning tea. Amy enjoyed the sessions greatly. She was never able to articulate the core doctrines of Christianity, nor did she 'say the sinner's prayer'. Yet I'm confident I'll see Amy again in glory because God in His gracious love brought her to faith through the Holy Spirit. Yes, Amy was living with significant cognitive decline, but conversion is deeper than cognition.

Important to this transformation are two realities:

- 'Spiritual growth is not simply possible in later life, it's likely.' —Elizabeth MacKinlay[10]

- People living with dementia can, and do, become Christians. As a chaplain, I see numerous conversions each year.[11]

Recognising the value of all people, and in light of Jesus' commandment to 'love your neighbour', it isn't enough just to say, 'we have a duty to love older people'. Scripture explicitly commands us to care for older people.[12]

For emphasis, let us consider four crucial verses regarding our treatment of older people:

Honour your father and your mother (Exod. 20:12, the Fifth Commandment).

You shall not mistreat any widow or fatherless child. If you do mistreat them, and they cry out to me, I will surely hear their cry, and my wrath will burn,

---

10 Elizabeth MacKinlay, keynote presentation at the 8th International Conference on Ageing and Spirituality, Canberra, 29 October 2019.

11 For an in-depth theology of people becoming Christians in the midst of dementia please read *Coming to Christ in Dementia* by Mark Wormell (Sydney, Mountain Stream Media, 2016) and *Ministry with the Forgotten: Dementia Through a Spiritual Lens*, by Kenneth L. Carder (Abingdon Press, 2019). A highly accessible way to examine some of the myths that have impeded the ministry of individual Christians, local churches and regional churches among older people is to view my video *Jesus Love in Aged Care 5 myths,* https://www.youtube.com/watch?v=CWHmkjRj_xU

12 To list just a few instances: Exodus 20:12, 22:22-24; Deuteronomy 10:18, 14:28-29, 15:11; Proverbs 28:27; Mark 12:40-44; 1 Timothy 5:1-24.

and I will kill you with the sword, and your wives
shall become widows and your children fatherless
(Exod. 22:22-24 ESV).

Love your neighbour as yourself (Mark 12:31, the
second half of Jesus' summary of how to live).

Religion that God our Father accepts as pure and
faultless is this: to look after orphans and widows in
their distress (James 1:27).

If you've been diligent and looked up all the above texts
(well done!), you will have noticed they primarily refer to
care for widows and parents. However, despite the view of
many teens, not all parents or widows are old. It's possible
to be both a parent and a widow in one's teens, and this

Dementia and Sin

Some people living with dementia report that Christians
have told them there is a causal link with their sin and
that repentance will result in them being healed.

While some dementias may have a behavioural link,
for example, Wernicke–Korsakoff dementia is typically
linked with excessive alcohol consumption and Dementia
Pugilistica is linked to head knocks (however, Dementia
Pugilistica can also be linked to domestic violence,
where, by definition, the person was a victim). Biblically,
dementia is generally the result of living in a broken world.
As such, while prayer is certainly a scriptural response to
dementia, and God can and does choose to miraculously
heal people, linking repentance and healing with regard
to dementia is unbiblical.

---

would have been more common in biblical times. As such, is it appropriate to apply these texts to older people?

While both widows and parents are not necessarily older, being older brings a higher probability of being both a parent and a widow (or widower). Moreover, in ancient times, widows typically remarried (e.g. Ruth 1:8 and 1 Tim. 5:14). So, while widows and parents can be younger, there's evidence that the majority of widows were older.

Before continuing, it's important to examine this commandment. First, there's no comment about the 'quality' of the parent or widow to determine whether or not they 'deserve' to be honoured. Scripture doesn't say we are to honour good parents, but all parents. This is significant, as I've seen children justify elder abuse because of pain or trauma they suffered at their parent's hands earlier in life.

> 'The poor, frail, broken, old and disabled are not primarily recipients in need of our care but our brothers and sisters'.
> —Stephen Pickard
>
> 'As The Third Alter' by Stephen Pickard in *Making the Word of God Fully Known: Essays on Church, Culture, and Mission in Honor of Archbishop Philip Freier*, eds. Barker, P. & Billings, B (Wipf & Stock, 2020).

There's a temptation to hear 'honour your parents' as primarily relating to children. However, to think we 'outgrow' this commandment is unbiblical. Indeed, there is strong evidence the commandment primarily applies to adult children. Specifically, the commandment itself has no age limit and none of the other commandments are limited to a particular life stage. Additionally,

Ephesians 6:1-3 makes it clear that honouring parents isn't just a command, but also a path to blessing. So again, while not all parents are older, many parents are.

I hasten to add that caring for older people, and particularly for those who have been or are abusive, is incredibly challenging. It requires wisdom, prayer and boundaries, and may also often include professional support, such as counselling.

'I don't want to miss a minute'

When I met Aline and Alf they had been married for sixty-six years and were living in a retirement village. Alf had advanced Alzheimer's and Aline was not simply his wife, but also his devoted carer.

Alf's increasing care needs were significantly impacting Aline's health. When I spoke with Aline and gently suggested she get more help or consider Alf moving into a dementia-specific unit she replied: 'Yes, it's tough, but dementia is a terminal condition. I know it will take Alf and I don't want to miss a minute with him'.

I haven't recorded this story to discount the value of a person moving into care. It's often the best option and allows family to be family, rather than cook, cleaner and nurse. I've included this story to emphasise the blessing of caring for a person living with dementia.

Second, is the commandment 'to honour' limited to 'your' parents and is 'widow' limited to older women (e.g. not widowers)? Certainly, Scripture teaches that Christians have a particular responsibility to care for our family members: 'But if anyone does not provide for his relatives, and especially for members of his household, he has denied the faith and is worse than an unbeliever.' (1 Tim. 5:8 ESV). However, Jesus was blunt in His response to people who limited commandments (Matt. 5 and Mark 7). It's clear Christians have a particular responsibility to care for older people generally. This is captured beautifully in the Westminster Larger catechism.[13]

It's a privilege

The preceding sections have emphasised the biblical imperative to love both older people and people living with dementia. However, love is never simply a commandment. It's also a privilege. Getting to know, learn from and engage with older people and people living with dementia is an incredible blessing. If we fail to engage, we not only lose an opportunity to serve, but also an opportunity to learn, to find inspiration and to challenge our faith.

Language

'Sticks and stones may break my bones, but words will never hurt me' is simply not true. Indeed, Scripture teaches about the power of words. For people who are older or who are living with dementia, words, even well-intentioned words, can cause significant harm.

---

13 **Question 124**: Who are meant by father and mother in the fifth commandment? **Answer**: By father and mother, in the fifth commandment, are meant, not only natural parents, but all superiors in age and gifts; and especially such as, by God's ordinance, are over us in place of authority, whether in family, church, or commonwealth.

With reference to dementia, unhelpful language includes: 'demented', which implies the disease is the person (we would not describe a person living with cancer as 'cancered');[14] 'dementia sufferer', which implies dementia and pain are inextricably linked; and language that describes, or suggests, that the changes faced by people impacted by dementia are synonymous with death, e.g. 'Mum died twice, once with dementia, then with cardiac failure'. These are all examples of language that harms people living with dementia, and best practice is to use the phrase 'living with dementia' despite it being a bit clunky.

When referring to older people, terms such as 'aged', 'elderly', 'old', 'senile', 'geriatric' and 'senior' are all considered ageist.[15] This isn't simply being PC or woke. It's driven by the recognition that 'othering'[16] older people contributes to discrimination and abuse. The problem is that, depending on your context, many of these terms may be standard. For example, in Australia, government-funded support for older people is called 'aged care', 'geriatrics' is a recognised branch of medicine, and 'elder abuse' is the official term for the abuse of older people. In this book I've striven to avoid language that could be seen

---

14 'Demented' also should not be used as an insult to disrespect a position or a person one disagrees with.

15 There are resources available around best practice language, but as they are websites I haven't noted them because they change.

16 'Othering' is the treatment of a group as different, and thus deserving of different (typically poor) treatment. For example, racism depicts difference on the basis of ancestry, which leads to people of that ancestry being treated worse than people of 'our' ancestry.

as ageist, and where I couldn't find better language I've tried to use a footnote to highlight my discomfort.

Final comments

Engaging with and caring for older people can be costly on many levels; it expends time, money and emotions. However, as Christians, we must seek to love people who are rich in years both as a response to their innate value and because we're commanded to do so.

Further resources[17]

Keeping Love Alive as Memories Fade: The 5 Love Languages and the Alzheimer's Journey, by Deborah Barr, Edward G. Shaw and Gary Chapman (Northfield Publishing, 2016).

Living in the Memories of God, by John Swinton (SCM Press, 2012).

Ministry with the Forgotten: Dementia Through a Spiritual Lens, by Kenneth L. Carder (Abingdon Press, 2019).

---

17 Please note, the 'Further resources' listed in this book are not exhaustive but serve as a starting point for readers to learn more.

2

Christian Love in the Context of Older People and People Living with Dementia

PART ONE

The Bible tells us that older people are of great value, they are much loved by God, and we are called to love them. In this chapter, we build on this foundational truth to examine the practicalities of how we can effectively care for older people and those living with dementia. Essentially, we need to practise the three Ps: prayer, presence and pastoral care.

Prayer

As God is the source of our ability to love, our whole lives need to start with, and be continually fuelled by, prayer. Just as, when starting a driving holiday, the fuel tank needs to be filled up and then regularly topped up along the way to power the trip, prayer is fuel for ministry. It's needed before, during and after all we undertake, to enable us to love. Even when we cannot physically visit, we can and should be praying.

Presence

Which brings us to our next 'P': Presence (aka turning up!). Too often, for reasons that may include fear of not knowing what to do and say, or because of the hectic pace of life, we can neglect to offer our presence. Yet our presence can be so valuable, particularly for older people and people living with dementia.

If, like me, you've ever gone door to door as part of church outreach, you will know that only a few people will answer the door let alone want to chat. By contrast, most older people are desperate for a chat, a hot drink and a connection with another person. However, it would be wrong to regard older people as a captive audience. The utmost tact and discretion are required to ensure that we're welcome and don't outstay our welcome, particularly with people who struggle to express their wishes verbally.

Confession

Describing 'presence' as simply turning up is an over simplification.

For example, when riding on public transport, particularly in an urban context, one is by definition physically present with many others but the etiquette is to minimise any other form of presence.

By contrast 'true' presence is about actively engaging with another person. Just as there are levels of listening, there are levels of presence and the deeper the level the more skill, effort and time that is required.

The good news is, irrespective of your current skill level, you can learn both to listen better and to be more present.

This requires great sensitivity and must never involve any form of coercion.

Moreover, if an older person is housebound (or care-home bound), and particularly if they're single, then how many people will they see each day? Even in a care home where they're likely to see several people, the staff are busy and other residents may be hard to relate to. In such a context, the value of a visitor, any visitor, is incredibly high. It's important to add a caveat here: a visit doesn't always need to be long (e.g. over an hour). Often (and particularly when visiting people with moderate to advanced dementia), multiple short visits may be more effective than extended visits.

Given the realities of distance and lockdowns due to infectious diseases it's important to recognise that our physical presence isn't always possible. Thankfully, we live in a time where we can employ a range of other options. The first is 'snail mail'. Everyone likes getting mail (except bills) so consider sending postcards, letters, goodies (e.g. reading

---

Time is Relative

If a person sleeps for nine hours and spends four hours per day on the necessities of daily life (e.g. dressing, eating and bathroom activities), there are eleven hours left.

If you're working full-time, then this isn't nearly enough. However, if you're retired, and particularly if you're retired and living with some level of frailty, then how do you spend all those hours (seventy-seven hours per week)?

material, sweets and nuts),[1] books and DVDs. I visited one resident whose son – who lived over twenty hours away by car – arranged for a box of fruit to be delivered to his mum each week. Not only did it increase her fruit intake, but it also gave her the opportunity to give to others – a double gift.

Another option is phone calls. These don't need to be long; indeed, my grandmother would stop most calls after two minutes with 'I know this is costing you' (despite multiple assurances that I had unlimited calls). A big advantage of a quick call is that I could make the call when I had a few spare minutes.

On the topic of phones, there are now a number of phones (both landline and mobile) designed for use by older people and people living with dementia. However, if an older person you're caring for doesn't have a phone and is in a care home, the home may have a phone they can take in to them.

Finally, there are a plethora of internet-based options such as email, WhatsApp and Zoom. I suggest to families that if their loved one can work an iPad, they might consider purchasing one so they can exchange texts, photos and videos. These allow the recipient the opportunity to reminisce and review their messages, and it can act as a 'brag book' to share with others. Additionally, staff may be able to assist with setting up video calls and may be able to print photos.

---

1   Please be aware that some people have dietary issues, for example allergies, swallowing difficulties and diabetes.

Pastoral care

I'm very aware 'pastoral care' can be intimidating (e.g. 'but I'm not a pastoral person') but basic Christian pastoral care isn't rocket science. It starts with a relationship with Jesus (we can't share what we don't have), is powered by prayer ('Lord, help me') and is typically expressed relationally (relationships normally start with our presence). So, if you've got this far through the book you're well on your way!

Perhaps it would therefore be helpful to examine some basics of pastoral care:

- Try to hear and reflect people's emotions. For example, 'It sounds like you're feeling sad/ frustrated/angry'. Please don't say, 'I know how you feel' – Jesus, who literally saw into people's hearts, didn't, so we certainly can't!

- When you visit someone don't feel you have to stay for an extended period. Short visits are often more effective than longer ones.

- Remember that not mentioning Jesus doesn't make a visit – or indeed multiple visits – worthless.

- Demonstrate His love by listening[2] and not by defending God.[3] Both presence and listening are active gifts, not passive ones.

---

2   Most people who are angry at God, are angry for emotional reasons, not logical ones. Listening, with empathy and without judgement, demonstrates God's love much more powerfully than telling people about God's love.

3   While I enjoy *apologetics* (defence of the faith), I know God doesn't need me to defend Him.

- Pastoral ministry is a marathon not a sprint, so please don't give up.

- Please prioritise self-care.[4] Burnout isn't a mark of success!

- Get help! Being willing to admit 'I don't know what to say' and referring someone to an expert is a sign of wisdom, not failure.

Having covered these basics, I strongly encourage everyone to continually seek to improve their pastoral and communication skills. Even the best communicators can improve, and both communication and pastoral care are life skills. The good news is that there are a range of great resources and courses aimed at improving pastoral skills and, as with everything else, 'practice makes perfect'.

While this list may seem scary, the 'to do' list is very simple: practise the three Ps.

1. Prayer.

2. Presence.

3. Pastoral care.

Friends, Jesus loves you and has empowered you to pray, turn up and love people. Jesus will use you when you pray, turn up and love people.

---

4   Please see the chapter entitled Boundaries (p. 81).

Further resources

'5 tips for engaging with older people', by Ben Boland, Youtube, 2025. (I have a number of video resources to complement this book available on my YouTube channel.)

Clinical Pastoral Education (CPE).

Spiritual Care Series, Health Television Network (https://htn.edu.au/spiritual-care-series/).

Worshipping with Dementia: Meditations, Scriptures and Prayers for Sufferers and Carers, by Louise Morse (Monarch Books, 2010).

3

Christian Love in the Context of Older People and People Living with Dementia

PART TWO

For many, the previous chapter may have been more of a refresher rather than new information. If that's you, thank you for your patience. In this section I want to delve into prayer, presence and pastoral care a bit more deeply to encourage, equip, and perhaps improve your ministry.

Prayer

The most significant lesson I received at Bible College was learning to pray. I grew up in a Christian home and can't remember a time when I didn't know Jesus' love. So, I'd been praying for decades before going to college, and I'd been regularly leading prayers in home groups and church contexts. However, at Bible College my prayer life reached a different level. It was not a result of greater biblical literacy, theology or doctrine (though these were all blessings that informed and improved my prayer life). Instead, it was the Puritan challenge to 'pray until you pray',[1] which I understand to mean to pray until you feel you're connecting with God.

Part of my problem was that I had a short attention span and was quite busy with family, church and college. I could pray for a few minutes but would then get distracted. The breakthrough came following advice from Stuart Coulton[2] who suggested I try walking and praying and, specifically, that I pray my way through the Psalms. I went from struggling to pray for five minutes to enjoying long and deep prayer times. As a chaplain, a key strategy for me is to walk around either the retirement village or care home praying.

Some people find a prayer journal helpful, while others use palm cards or devotional booklets. Traditionally, prayer beads and labyrinths are tools some people find helpful.

Another strategy I've found particularly helpful is using the Anglican Prayer Book.[3] I picked this up from

---

1   D. A. Carson, *Praying with Paul: A Call to Spiritual Reformation* (Baker Academic, 2015), p. 17.

2   Stuart Coulton was the deputy principal and went on to be the principal of Sydney Missionary and Bible College (SMBC).

3   If you're not familiar with the Anglican Prayer Book, it's a bit of a living document as different prayer books have been developed across the world and over time. Typically, the Anglican Prayer Books have long names that are abbreviated. For example, the original Anglican Prayer Book is *The Book of Common Prayer* (BCP). In the Australian context *An Australian Prayer Book* (AAPB) was published in 1978 and *A Prayer Book for Australia* in 1995 (APBA). All these prayer books are scripturally based, but the understanding of Scripture varies according to the theology of the authors. It's worth nothing that, if you're ministering to older Anglicans, an appropriate Prayer Book may be a powerful tool.

a minister who said that he reaches for it when he's struggling to pray. Some people feel that praying written formal prayers feels less holy, too formal or not 'Spirit-led'. Personally, I believe a healthy prayer life should include both written and extemporary prayers as Jesus gave His disciples a 'formal' prayer but also prayed extemporarily (e.g. John 17). Additionally, Scripture records numerous other prayers and the Psalms that serve us as 'formal' prayers. The danger of only praying formally is thinking the words are 'magic'; the danger of only praying extemporarily is a lack of the depth and reflection that comes from having to think, reflect and wrestle when writing a prayer.

In terms of resources for formal prayers I love to use Scripture: The Psalms, the Lord's Prayer and other prayers from the Bible. I also strongly recommend *Praying with Paul: A Call to Spiritual Reformation*.[4]

> 'I believe that there is no-one of whom it can be said that the Spirit of God cannot penetrate their troubled mind.'
> —Neville Chamberlain, *In A Strange Land*, p. 1

On the topic of praying the words[5] and ideas of the Bible,[6] I don't limit myself to passages I've memorised

---

4 D. A. Carson, *Praying with Paul: A Call to Spiritual Reformation* (Baker Academic, 2015).

5 For example, praying the psalms – 'My good shepherd, please not only be with me, but may I know your presence as I walk in the shadow of death' (Ps. 23).

6 For example, praying about creation – 'Father thank you for the amazing world you created and sustain. For the scent of roses and the feel of grass under my feet.'

(though memorising Scripture is wonderful). I seek to pray through the Bible stories. For example, consider the macro events of Genesis (e.g. creation, the fall and the flood) and take time to pray through them. Even better, learn the micro stories and pray through them.[7]

However, I also seek to draw on the riches of church history to shape my prayers. For example, my prayer 'toolbox' includes: *The Valley of Vision*,[8] old hymn books and an *Anglican Prayer Book*.

Presence

At its most basic, presence is intentional silence. Not simply a lack of noise but being actively focused on the other person. For me, presence starts with theology, specifically a desire to love the other person and the belief that God doesn't need me to speak. Please also note that intentional presence is exhausting.

I'm not advocating simply 'preaching the gospel at all times and sometimes using words' because Jesus often used words.

I want to emphasise that presence needs to be learnt. Indeed, the old saying 'practice makes perfect' is very true. I suspect introverts have a natural advantage as they feel less need to speak or have other people's attention

---

7   By 'micro stories' I mean the accounts of the 'little' people – 'Lord, may I be faithful when I am faced with immoral imperatives from the government, as Shiphrah and Puah were' (Exod. 1). There is also value in praying though single events in the lives of the 'heroes of the faith' – 'Jesus help me as I face conflict within the church just as Paul and Barnabas faced conflict' (Acts 15).

8   Arthur Bennett, *The Valley of Vision* (Banner of Truth Trust, 1975).

but, irrespective of our personality, we all need to work to develop our presence.

If this was simply a book about pastoral care I would suggest a 'verbatim-writing' exercise. This would involve trainees recording a pastoral encounter like a play script including both what was said and 'stage notes'.[9] Your task would be to reflect on the encounter individually and with a mentor. This is the methodology used in *Clinical Pastoral Education* (*CPE*) and it's the best way I know of learning advanced listening skills.[10]

It's also best practice to have a pastoral supervisor who can help you hone your presence. We'll return to the topic of pastoral supervision later in this book.

Finally, presence is particularly important for people with delirium[11] and some people with dementia whose reality is different from those around them. In such circumstances simply being present can be profoundly powerful.

Pastoral care – a theological reflection

Pastoral care is a contested space as this term is sometimes used to refer simply to the gentle care of people, particularly those in distress. This definition means proponents of diverse world views, faith or no faith, can all provide

---

9   For example: Ben: 'Good morning George.' George: 'Hi Ben, can I tell you something?' (George appeared distressed and was wringing his hands.)

10 In Australia and the US, *CPE* has faced criticism because it doesn't grade participants, so it has been superseded by courses that do.

11 *Delirium* is where a person's brain in not working well for a short time. Deliriums are commonly experienced by older people, and they're highly treatable.

pastoral care. The problem with this usage is that the word 'pastoral' comes from the Christian tradition and entails significantly more than just 'being nice'.

Certainly, Christianity isn't unique in caring for people but, while care of people is currently culturally popular, it's not a universal cultural norm. For example, the early church was very countercultural as it cared for both discarded infants and impoverished older people who were neither Christians nor family members.[12]

I'm not simply arguing that the term 'pastoral care' has been appropriated. My concern is to clarify the meaning of pastoral care. Christian pastoral care (henceforth 'pastoral care') comes from the biblical imagery of God as the good shepherd and the commandment for church leaders to shepherd the church.

The challenge is that the only shepherds seen in most of the Western world today are in nativity scenes. No, sorry I'm wrong. Sheepdogs have a long heritage and there's an increasing use of shepherd animals in agriculture (alpacas, donkeys and herd-protection/guardian dogs).[13] The job of these animals is to protect the flock from predators, such as foxes and wild dogs. They do this by being with the flock (presence), and warning and attacking predators (pastoral care).

Likewise, first-century shepherds were constantly with the flock (presence), they guided the flock to good food and water and protected the flock at the risk of their own

---

12   More information about this can be found in *Bullies and Saints: An Honest Look at the Good and Evil of Christian History*, by John Dickson (Zondervan Reflective, 2021), pp. 80-83.

13   Herding sheepdogs are used to move sheep whereas herd protection dogs protect the flock from predators.

lives (Ps. 23; John 10). Shepherding was hard, rough and not a job with significant prestige. In 1 Samuel 16, we see the shepherd (Jesse's youngest son, David) isn't even significant enough to be called to the feast that was held for Samuel, the great prophet of the day.

However, the primary lesson is that pastoral care derives from God's love for people and is a manifestation of our love for both God and people. This is important as there's a huge difference between being loving and being nice. Yes, in terms of action, nice and love can sometimes look similar. But nice neither lays down its life for nor challenges a person.

Jesus, our model of pastoral care, not only used words a lot, but He also used challenging words (e.g. Matt. 12). Even when Jesus was dealing with very broken people, He could be quite direct: 'The fact is, you have had five husbands, and the man you now have is not your husband. What you have just said is quite true' (John 4). I'm not suggesting pastoral care is just challenging words – Jesus' words were often incredibly gentle. However, to suggest that pastoral care has no hard edges is simply not biblical.

Further resources

Bullies and Saints: An Honest Look at the Good and Evil of Christian History, by John Dickson (Zondervan Reflective, 2021).

Still Waters Run Deep: Theological Reflections on Dementia, Faithfulness and Peaceable Presence, edited by John Swinton and Elizabeth MacKinlay (Routledge, 2024).

4

Sharing Jesus' Love in the Midst of Dementia

How can we effectively share Jesus with people living with dementia who don't already know His love for them? Before we turn to this important question, let me address two common myths.

Myth One: It's abusive to present Jesus to people living with dementia who are not in relationship with Him.

Response: Jesus clearly taught that relationship with God (both now and eternal), is available to all who believe. Jesus clearly calls *all* people to repent, believe and follow Him, and He calls Christians to share this message with others. To exclude any group of people from hearing this

'Spiritual growth is not simply possible in later life, it's likely.'
—Elizabeth MacKinlay
Keynote address, 29 October 2019, 8th International Conference on Ageing and Spirituality Canberra

'good news' is unbiblical. However, I'm not suggesting (nor does Scripture support) 'Bible bashing'[1]

Myth Two: People living with moderate to advanced dementia cannot become Christians.

Response: I don't expect a person living with moderate to advanced dementia to be able to write a 5,000-word essay on Penal Substitutionary Atonement. For some Christians, such an exercise is profoundly helpful, but they are in the minority. Friends, becoming a Christian isn't simply a cognitive exercise but a spiritual and relational one. Scripture is clear: God can and does save people, and not simply through their minds.[2] I regularly see people living with mild, moderate and advanced dementia come to faith as evidenced by their love for God and neighbour.

> 'Our reluctance to question or challenge older people may subtly remove them from the human race. It pretends, in effect, that they're moral non-entities; it treats them condescendingly as though they were toys. We will take an important step towards re-entry into community with the aged when we are willing to attend to them seriously enough as moral beings to approve and reprove their behaviour.'
> —William F. May, 'The Virtues and Vices of the Elderly', in *What Does It Mean to Grow Old?* (Duke University Press, 1986), p. 43.

---

1 'Bible bashing' being trying to coerce a person to convert.

2 If you're interested in the theology behind faith in the midst of dementia, I recommend *Coming to Christ in Dementia* by Mark Wormell (Mountain Stream Media, 2016).

Having established that Christians are called to share the good news of Jesus with people living with dementia, let's explore the practicalities. We start by returning to the three Ps: Prayer, Presence and Pastoral care. These are the basics. However, as Christians, we should be building on these basics in terms of looking to verbally express Jesus' love, not simply to model and practise it. Too often I hear Christians say 'I want my actions to be so powerful I never have to use words'. Jesus used words regularly! To be like Jesus is to speak of Jesus' love, to tell stories from the Gospels, to tell stories from history (e.g. John Newton and 'Amazing Grace'; Corrie ten Boom and forgiveness; Susanna Wesley and prayer), and to tell stories of how God has touched our lives.

Like Jesus, we need to be highly sensitive to the people we're engaging with. Jesus' words were tailored to His audience. For example, the way Jesus spoke to Nicodemus in John 3 is profoundly different from the way He spoke to the woman at the well in John 4. While each person is different, and therefore every person living with dementia is also different, I've found these generalisations to be helpful in effectively communicating with those living with dementia. Be careful not to underestimate a person's ability to understand, while also seeking to tailor your communication to the person you're with.

- Short is better than long.

- Concrete is better than abstract. For example, generally it's better to share a story of Jesus' life from the Gospels, rather than to try to explain the theology of Hebrews.

- Meet the person where they are, not where you want them to be.[3]

- Consider and engage all the senses (taste, touch, smell, sound and sight).[4]

- Repetition is powerful but can be overdone.

- Simple, never simplistic.[5]

- Look and pray for opportunities but don't 'force it'. We share Jesus' love; we don't coerce people into loving Jesus.

These guidelines can be implemented in three overlapping ways: informally, formally and creatively.

Informally

When someone asks 'What did you do on the weekend?', do you mention church and how it touched you? If so, you're sharing Jesus' love informally. Indeed, sharing Jesus' love informally is simply about looking for opportunities to share how Jesus has, and Jesus is, impacting your life. Of course, wisdom and tact are needed. Forcing God into every conversation isn't biblical, nor did Jesus talk only

---

3   For example, you may desperately want to continue your last conversation about the power of the Holy Spirit, but the person wants to reminisce about their garden – so reminisce!

4   For more information consider the chapters on multisensory ministry (p. 39, 49).

5   While dementia and aged care ministry can look and at times feel very similar to children's ministry, the HUGE difference is older people and people living with dementia are not children! Also, not even children enjoy being talked down to. We must be careful to never patronise older people.

about faith, hope and love.[6] So, we don't need to 'force it' but, equally, we need to be looking (and praying) for opportunities and the right words. Trusting God means that those who are shy can rely on Him to help them be bold and speak. For others, trusting God means 'shutting up' in the certainty it's God who saves, not us!

> 'In the same way that we encourage people in our care to explore and engage with new activities and interests, holistic care must encourage new spiritual activities and interests'.
> —Andrew Cameron

Formally

Formal ways of sharing Jesus' love are simply events that are focused on Jesus' love, for example church services,[7] Bible studies and Bible reading groups.[8] But please don't

---

6   For example: Matthew 8:1-17, 20:29-30; Mark 1:29-34, 1:40-45, 7:31-37, 8:22-28, 10:46-52; Luke 5:12-16, 7:11-17, 17:11-18; John 5:1-15.

7   Church services are covered in more detail in the chapter Church and Preaching. (p. 103)

8   There's growing evidence of the therapeutic value of reading. For example, see: *Bibliotherapy*, McNicol, S., & Brewster, L. (eds.) (Facet, 2018); *Bibliotherapy*, by Karges-Bone, Dr L. (Lorenz Educational Press, 2015), https://bibliotherapyaustralia.com.au/. A Bible reading group is simply a group that gathers together to listen to the Bible. Sometimes it includes a discussion (similar to a book club), but not always. The value of reading groups is particularly high in the context of older persons and those living with dementia as many of them are no longer able to read due to vision impairment, arthritis and shaking (e.g. Parkinson's). From a Christian perspective, the importance of being able to access Scripture is hard to overstate.

be limited to these simple (but worthwhile) ideas. The most effective outreach I've ever been involved in within a care home was run by a volunteer who was passionate about women's ministry. She organised a ladies-only high tea three times a year, and included female Christian speakers and female Christian musicians. Each high tea had a theme, perfumed invitations, and a small gift for each woman present. The care home had approximately 120 female residents but there were never fewer than 150 women in attendance as the residents often invited daughters, granddaughters, great-granddaughters and female friends as guests.

Other effective strategies[9] include evangelistic short courses, seasonal Bible studies (e.g. for Lent and Advent), spiritual reminiscence[10] and Christmas Carols. There are also resources that are specifically designed for sharing Jesus' love with people living with moderate to advanced dementia.[11]

Creatively

No, I don't expect you to be a creative genius! I just mean we can use art, craft and music to effectively share Jesus' love with people living with dementia. For example, we can offer to read (Scripture, a devotional or hymn) or, even better, to sing a well-known hymn, as childhood

---

9   If you want more details please see the chapter entitled 'Practical Multisensory Ministry', p. 47.

10 *Facilitating Spiritual Reminiscence for People Living with Dementia: A Learning Guide,* by Elizabeth MacKinlay and Corinne Trevitt (Jessica Kingsley Publishers, 2015).

11 *Jesus Loves Me,* Ben Boland and Dana Gruben (HammondCare, 2020).

memories and music are often left intact by dementia. You could make a Resurrection Garden[12] and talk about Easter, or send a Christmas card that shares a message of hope.[13]

I hope you're eager to share Jesus' love with someone you know who's living with dementia. My prayer is that God will powerfully use your witness and your words. My final encouragement is to pray before, during and after every visit.

Figure 1: Resurrection Garden

---

12   See Figure 1 and Google 'Resurrection Garden'.

13   While your opportunities are only limited by your imagination, you may find Pinterest and the chapter 'Practical Multisensory Ministry' provide inspiration. The Appendix outlines the practicalities of setting up a multisensory garden designed for people living with dementia (p. 121).

Further resources

Coming to Christ in Dementia by Mark Wormell (Mountain Street Media, 2016).

'Dementia Chaplaincy' by Ben Boland in *The Heart of a Chaplain*, second edition, (eds) Jim Browning and Jim Spivey (Iron Stream Media, 2025)

Facilitating Spiritual Reminiscence for People Living with Dementia: A Learning Guide, by Elizabeth MacKinlay and Corinne Trevitt (Jessica Kingsley Publishers, 2015).

Messy Vintage: 52 sessions to share Christ-centred fun and fellowship with the older generation, by Katie Norman and Jill Phipps (Bible Reading Fellowship, 2021).

5

A Theology of
Multisensory Ministry

Is it reasonable to play the exquisite, powerful and saving music of the gospel in a pitch outside a person's hearing, and to expect them to join the chorus praising their Saviour? Even for people who have five perfect senses, failing to engage any of their senses with the gospel is limiting. For people living with partial or profound sensory loss (e.g. many older people and people living with dementia), not communicating in a multisensory manner can leave people without access to the gospel. This chapter provides a foray into a theology of gospel ministry within the context of sensory loss and provides practical suggestions to enhance gospel ministry generally.

Understanding sensory loss requires an examination of four major points. First, sensory losses impact all five senses. Compared to the other senses, taste may appear irrelevant; however, it's worth noting that a major area of complaint amongst people living in care homes is the food. Second, sensory loss can be either partial or total. Third, many people experience multiple sensory losses. Finally, there are significant indirect causes of sensory loss. For example, a person with perfect sensory physiology who is confined to a wheelchair (even an electric one) can experience sensory limitations due to its battery life. Or they may experience physical barriers such as the lack of access ramps, making it difficult for them to get up steps into a church building.

It's therefore clear that sensory loss is diverse in terms of which sense or senses are affected, the level of its impact (i.e. whether the loss is partial or total), and whether the cause of the sensory loss is direct or indirect (i.e. a loss of hearing or the ability to go upstairs to attend a meeting).

Having examined sensory loss, it's vital to note the impact of sensory loss on people both physically and spiritually. Biomedically, sensory loss leads to psychosocial distress, decreased communication, depression, anxiety, lethargy and social dissatisfaction.[1] Christianity has a strong history of caring for the suffering and a clear biblical imperative to do so. Additionally, all people need to hear the gospel. Romans 10:14 emphasises the salvific implication of not 'hearing' ('how can they believe in the one of whom they have not heard?'). Given that Paul wrote these words, which required sight to read the text 'hear',[2] it's fair to say that hearing relates to more than the ability to audibly 'hear'. Sensory loss has a profound effect on people's health, both biologically and spiritually.

---

1   *Spiritual Care with People Living with Sensory Loss*, by Ben Boland and Jeffery Cohen (forthcoming)

2   Or, more technically, 'sight to read'.

Finally, it is hard to conceive of a church that does not engage with all the senses. For example, unless the sermon is via podcast or the preacher stands behind a curtain, the preaching will contain a visual element. Communion is a multisensory sacrament. Indeed, if the church is first and foremost a gathering of believers, it will be multisensory, as people are designed to be multisensory.

Multisensory ministry in church history

Having recognised the impact of sensory loss, there's value in reflecting on how Christians have engaged with all five senses throughout church history. Catholic and Orthodox traditions have emphasised multisensory spirituality using incense, icons and statues, practices that can be uncomfortable for reformed evangelicals, who have prioritised Word ministry and faith over ceremony, and focus on the dangers of idolatry. Unequivocally, God is primarily revealed through Scripture, the gospel is based on faith alone, and idolatry remains a sin. Nevertheless, to discard anything except Word ministry is questionable. To use a musical analogy, these doctrines are the melody but adding other parts in harmony creates a richer sound.

Even within the reformed evangelical tradition, this isn't a new concept: worship is music for the ears; posture is touch in motion (e.g. sitting, standing and kneeling); Communion involves both smell and taste; images accompany and highlight the gospel (e.g. flowers, PowerPoint and colouring for children). This isn't surprising as it's almost impossible to live, let alone communicate, without engaging multiple senses. However, as the Bible is the rule for Christianity, we need to examine whether Scripture supports engaging all the senses in gospel ministry.

Multisensory ministry in the Old Testament

The Old Testament supports the argument for biblical ministry being multisensory in three major ways.

First, creation presents humans as physical beings with five God-created senses. Furthermore, God describes humans, people with five senses, as 'very good'. Thus, all five senses are both God-given and good.

Second, idolatry via graven images was a perpetual sin in the Old Testament, leading Puritans to destroy stained glass windows and images. Idolatry remains a sin today. However, we can't assume that the removal of images equates to a removal of idolatry; this is dangerous because Scripture doesn't limit idolatry to images.[3]

Finally, God-ordained Israelite worship was multisensory rather than exclusively Word-based. For example:

- Bible reading,[4] singing and instruments for the ear.[5]

- Incense[6] and the scent of sacrifices[7] filling the nose.

- Bitter herbs, lamb and unleavened bread on the tongue.[8]

---

3   Ephesians 5:5; Colossians 3:5.

4   Exodus 24:3; Deuteronomy 31:9-13; Joshua 8:34-35; 2 Kings 23:1-3; Nehemiah 8:1-8.

5   Exodus 15:1-21; Numbers 21:17; Psalms; Ezra 2:65; Zephaniah 3:14-17.

6   Exodus 30:1-10, 37:25-29.

7   Genesis 4:4; Exodus 9: 23-27, 15:9-20; Leviticus 1.

8   Exodus 12.

- Rich colours, movement, and decoration in the Tabernacle[9] and Temple[10] for the eye.

- Circumcision,[11] Sabbath rest,[12] building the booths[13] and anointing with oil[14] are all tactile experiences.

Therefore, it's clear that godly Old Testament spirituality engaged all the senses. Unequivocally, Word ministry was pivotal. However, it was not Word without the other senses, both in terms of overt worship (see above) and in terms of life generally, such as caring for the poor, eating and agricultural practices. While Old Testament worship emphasised reading God's Word, preaching and prophecy, it also embraced the use of the other senses.

The question therefore becomes, does this apply to God's people post-crucifixion? This is significant as practices such as temple worship and circumcision were supplanted by the new covenant.

Multisensory ministry in the New Testament

Not only that, but all five of the senses are God-given and good. When Jesus became human, He experienced touch, sight, taste, smell and sound. Indeed, Jesus' life and ministry were overtly multisensory. For example:

---

9   Exodus 25–29; 35–38.

10 1 King 6–7; 2 King 18:15.

11 Exodus 24:4-7.

12 Exodus 20:9-11, 23:3 ; Deuteronomy 5:12-15.

13 Exodus 23:33-43.

14 Leviticus 8:30; Exodus 28:41; 1 Samuel 10:1.

- The scent of Jesus' feet being perfumed engages the sense of smell.[15]

- The descent of the dove,[16] the calming of the storm[17] and the raising of the dead[18] are all visual.

- The changing of water into to wine,[19] feeding the multitudes[20] and meals with His disciples[21] all attest to Jesus' use of taste and smell.

- Jesus' refrain 'let those who have ears'[22] highlights the importance Jesus placed on physical and spiritual hearing.

- Jesus touched the untouchable,[23] said 'let the little children come to me,'[24] and, after the resurrection, told Thomas to touch His hands and side.[25]

Clearly, Jesus ministered in a multisensory manner, but is this just a function of His incarnation or is it prescriptive for Christians?

---

15 Matthew 26; Mark 14; Luke 7; John 12.

16 Matthew 3; Mark 1; Luke 3; John.

17 Matthew 8; Mark 4; Luke 8; John 6.

18 Mark 5; Luke 7; John 11.

19 John 2.

20 Matthew 14; Mark 6; Luke 9; John 6.

21 Matthew 9, 12, 14–15, 26; Mark 2, 6, 8, 14; Luke 5–7, 9–11, 14, 22, 24; John 2, 6, 12–13, 21.

22 Matthew 11:33; Mark 4; Luke 8, 14.

23 Matthew 8; Luke 5.

24 Matthew 19; Luke 18; Mark 10.

25 Luke 24; John 20.

Firstly, given Jesus' sinless nature, it is impossible to argue multisensory ministry is sinful.

Secondly, Jesus' incarnation is significant because we too are human, we too have a physical body and five senses.[26]

Thirdly, while Jesus is totally exceptional[27] and His primary purpose was to die for the sins of the world, there is strong biblical support for Jesus also being our model for life and ministry – and Jesus' ministry was intentionally multisensory.[28]

Given Jesus' ministry was so multisensory, the question becomes: why would we not seek to be multisensory in our ministry too?

Three primary objections to focusing on multisensory ministry are: idolatry, pre-eminence of Word ministry and resources. These are all critical risk factors – as multisensory ministry could lead to idolatry, diminishment of Word ministry and take limited resources away from other critical areas. However, risks are not limited to multisensory ministry. For example, Scripture is risky in that it can be taken out of context and sermons may contain heresy, but engaging with Scripture and preaching are biblical commandments. Therefore, all ministry needs to include theologically robust risk management.

We see evidence of this in letters of the New Testament which record the church being deliberately multisensory – Baptism,[29] Communion,[30] the laying on of hands (e.g.

---

26 Yes, as previously noted many people have sensory impairment(s).

27 Fully God and fully human.

28 1 Corinthians 11.

29 Acts 2, 8, 22; Romans 6; Galatians 3; 1 Peter 3.

30 Acts 2; 1 Corinthians 11.

for healing[31] and ordination[32]) and the miracles recorded in Acts are all multisensory – while also managing risks to ministry. For example, the condemnation of Ananias and Sapphira[33] and the warnings against false teachers[34] are not commandments *not* to give financially or to teach, but to do so in a biblical manner.

Additionally, Paul's description of a 'fragrant offering'[35] echoes Old Testament descriptions of God's sense of smell. The use of visual language in the Gospel of John and the Letter of James – shadow, light and darkness – highlights the importance of multisensory ministry. For people who are living with sensory loss, a mono-sensory approach is crippling.

Therefore, I would argue the question is not, should the church use multisensory ministry, but, how should we be intentionally multisensory in our ministry in a church service and beyond?

Further resources

Spiritual Care with People Living with Sensory Loss, by Ben Boland and Jeffery Cohen (forthcoming).

Music Remembers Me: Connection and Wellbeing in dementia, by Kirsty Beilharz (HammondCare, 2017).

---

31 1 Timothy 5; James 5.

32 1 Timothy 4–5.

33 Acts 5.

34 1 Timothy 4.

35 Ephesians 5; Philippians 4.

6

Practical Multisensory Ministry

Having demonstrated the biblical importance of multi-sensory ministry, it's helpful to outline some examples of multisensory ministry with older adults or people living with dementia. Growing up in an Evangelical tradition I was not even aware of the existence of any Christian seasonal events other than Easter and Christmas. However, as a chaplain I see them as great opportunities to share Jesus' love.

The following lists seven seasonal events you may be able to use in your ministry with older people and those living with dementia:

- Lent
- Easter
- Pentecost
- St Patrick's Day
- Harvest

- Advent
- Christmas

Lent

Lent is the six weeks leading up to Easter. Like Easter, the dates vary each year, and it's historically a time of fasting (giving up something) and prayer.

Shrove Tuesday

The Tuesday before Lent is called Shrove Tuesday or Pancake Day. Lent was traditionally a time of fasting and, in the Western church,[1] Shrove Tuesday developed as a celebration and a way of using up perishable rich food. Cooking pancakes became the customary way to eat up eggs, milk and sugar.

This tradition is easy to replicate within a care home context by serving pancakes and including a short talk about Lent and Easter. It's an opportunity to have people participate in making the pancake batter, watching the cooking (using an electric frying pan or barbecue) and enjoying the pancakes together. In terms of fasting, many churches that mark Lent today encourage their parishioners to give up or take up something. Personally, I typically encourage people to use Lent as a time to read one of the Gospels.

Ash Wednesday

Ash Wednesday (the day after Shrove Tuesday) marks the start of Lent. It's traditionally celebrated with a church

---

1   The Eastern Orthodox churches also fast during Lent but the very devout give up different foods at different points during Lent.

service during which the minister uses ashes[2] to make the sign of the cross on the heads of the congregants.[3]

There's a clear link here with the call to repentance and the Old Testament practice of using sackcloth and ashes as a sign of confession.[4] However, the practicalities of having two Lenten events back-to-back is a challenge both for organisers and for many older people and people living with dementia. Therefore, I suggest celebrating either Shrove Tuesday or Ash Wednesday and, in my experience, pancakes are more of a draw than ash crosses, especially for people who may not be regular churchgoers.

Lenten Bible study

As Lent is a short season and Easter is the high point of the Christian calendar, it's an ideal time to run a six-week Bible study series. There are good Bible study resources[5] you can use, or you could consider partnering with a local church to run the study.

Posters

Consider making your own posters either as a craft activity or on your computer (for an example see Figure 2).[6]

---

2   The ash comes from the burnt palms used to decorate the church from the previous year's Palm Sunday.

3   This tradition continues in some Anglican and Catholic churches.

4   Numbers 5:7; Leviticus 5:5; Psalm 32:1; James 5:16; 1 John 1:9.

5   For example, *I saw a Lamb: The Cross in Revelation*, Michael Raiter (Anglican Press Australia, 2020). Also, *Studies for Lent and Other Times – Ephesus and the New Humanity: A call to reignite the church's passion for Christ*, by Reg Piper (Anglican Press Australia, 2010).

6   These posters can be created for a range of seasonal ministries (e.g. Christmas, Easter and Advent) as well as to promote events and activities.

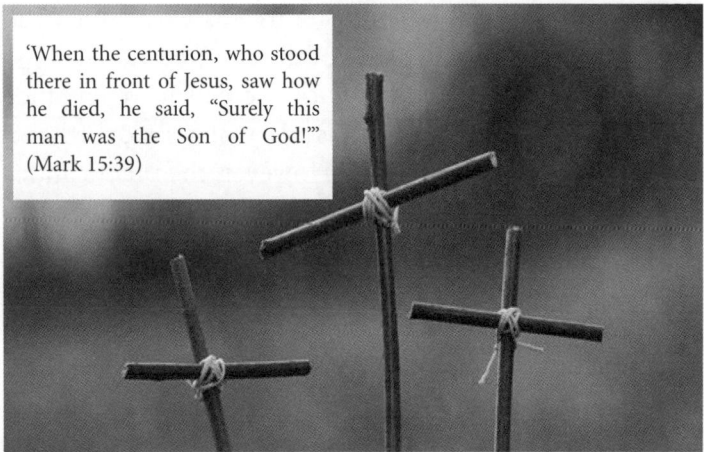

'When the centurion, who stood there in front of Jesus, saw how he died, he said, "Surely this man was the Son of God!"' (Mark 15:39)

Figure 2: DIY Easter

Palm crosses

Traditionally given out on Palm Sunday, palm crosses (crosses made from folded palm leaves, see Figure 3) are a great gift for congregation members to take home or to give to their neighbours. Palm crosses can be purchased but are not hard to make and are a great Easter craft activity.

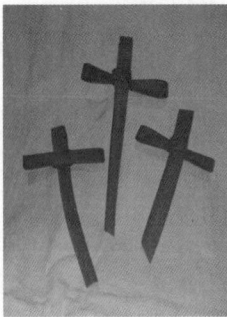

Figure 3: Palm Crosses

Easter services

Traditionally there are four key Easter church services: Palm Sunday – celebrating Jesus' entry into Jerusalem; Maundy Thursday – remembering the Last Supper; Good Friday – focusing on the crucifixion; and Easter Sunday – celebrating Jesus' resurrection.

With regard to special Easter Sunday services for older people and people living with dementia, the challenge for many churches and clergy is busyness. Additionally, Easter services often attract the largest congregations of the year because people come to church who don't normally attend. As a result, many churches see Easter as an important opportunity to connect with 'new' congregants.

Certainly, if resources permit, it's great to conduct additional care home and dementia-friendly church services. Alternatively, consider having at least one Easter service designed to be accessible to older people and people living with dementia.

My experience has been that Maundy Thursday is an ideal time to hold such a service because, as it's on a weekday, it's less likely to be attended by people with paid jobs or at school.

As Maundy Thursday commemorates the Last Supper, common elements of the service are Communion and foot washing.[7]

Pentecost

Pentecost (also known as Whitsunday) recalls the outpouring of the Holy Spirit as recorded in Acts 2. Celebrated fifty days after Easter it moves dates with Easter. In terms of multisensory ministry, traditional symbols have included the colour red (symbolising joy

---

7   When considering how best to make church services care home and dementia friendly, please see the final two chapters of this book: 'Church and Preaching' and 'Communion: Theology and Practice.'

and the Holy Spirit) and paper doves (symbolising the giving of the Holy Spirit).

St Patrick's Day

We all know St Patrick's Day is a day for celebrating all things Irish (e.g. wearing green, Guinness and Irish entertainment). The story of St Patrick is perhaps less well known.

St Patrick was an English boy who was captured by pirates and sold as a slave in Ireland. He eventually escaped and returned to England. After a few years he then returned to Ireland to share the good news of Jesus with the Irish. Although it's unlikely that he was the first 'missionary' to Ireland, it's clear that he had a profound impact on the people of Ireland, many of whom came to know Jesus.

St Patrick's Day is a beautiful combination of joyful celebration and gospel opportunity. Consider having a St Patrick's Day church service or incorporating some explicitly Christian components into a St Patrick's Day celebration. It goes without saying that there should be lots of green and possibly Guinness-tasting as part of the day![8]

Harvest

Traditionally Harvest church services focused on giving thanks for God's provision. Traditional elements include decorating the church building with food. Where possible I recommend trying to use local or regional produce. On

---

8   Please be aware some people require fluids to be a specific thickness to prevent choking and aspiration.

a practical note, if you want to use grains as part of the service, it's easiest to source and keep a sheaf of wheat or barley specially for the occasion as these aren't always harvested when you want them. The particular value of celebrating Harvest in a care home context is as a reminder to give thanks, which can prove challenging for people facing some of the common trials of ageing.

Advent

The liturgical season of Advent is traditionally a time when Christians remember Jesus' coming. It looks forward to His humble birth in Bethlehem and His Second Coming when He will return in power to judge the heavens and the earth.

For those who love words, *Advent* is derived from the Latin word *adventus*, which in turn was a translation of the Greek word *Parousia*. *Advent*, *Adventus*, and *Parousia* all mean *coming*.

This brings up the topic of word games as a form of multisensory ministry. Specifically, there's great value in creating a handout for seasonal celebration. I recommend including a Bible reading, hymn and prayer but also an image and a word game.[9] I include an image because, when leading from the front, I can say 'please turn to the page with the dove and we will sing *Amazing Grace*'. A word game has a triple function. First, it highlights the Bible passages as I use words from the Bible reading. Second, I encourage people to take the whole sheet home

---

9   There are a number of free websites where you enter words and it produces find-a-word, word search or crossword puzzles.

with them to complete the word game. Finally, it gives people something to do while gathering or leaving.

It's important to mark Advent because it leads up to the second most important event in the Christian calendar. Thankfully there are a number of effective, creative and practical ways to do so.

Advent decorations

Advent decorations are a challenge, not due to a lack of options but because of a culture clash. For Christians Advent is all about Christ, while in modern Western culture Christmas is primarily about family and Santa. People on both sides of this debate can be very passionate and intolerant of the other side. My suggestion is to display a mixture of Christian and secular decorations in general care home spaces (e.g. reception, halls, and dining rooms) and only Christian material in chapel spaces.

Below are some suggestions for Advent decorations.

Advent posters

Advent posters are quick, easy and cheap Advent decorations. They can easily be made on a computer and printed in A3 (ideally in colour).[10] There is a range of free Advent and Christmas images available online and I typically add a short Bible quote or piece from a carol or hymn to provide the text.

Advent calendars

There are numerous commercial Advent calendars. However, my personal favourite is a large Advent calendar

---

10 See Figure 2 as an example.

made using brown paper bags hung from string. One side of each bag has a number (counting down to Christmas Day) and the other a letter. The numbers countdown to Christmas Day, and when all the letters are revealed they spell out an Advent message. Each bag can be 'loaded' with a sweet, a gift and a Bible passage.

Figure 4:
Advent Calendars

Advent wreaths

While Advent is an ancient tradition that dates back to the third or fourth century, Advent wreaths originated in Germany in 1839. Since then they've evolved and changed to the point there's no 'correct' Advent wreath but rather a number of options. The basics are an evergreen wreath symbolising life (in the Northern Hemisphere Advent falls in winter) and a number of candles (between four and twenty-four). Ordinarily just four candles are used, with one being lit on each Sunday in Advent. The meaning of each candle can easily be found online so I'll just focus on the practicalities.

As wax candles pose a fire risk, electronic candles are a good alternative. However, it can be challenging and expensive to source candles of the right colour and size. One solution is to place cheap electric tea lights into wax candles thus getting the best of both worlds. Electric candles also make it easier for the Advent wreath to be moved from wherever the church services are held to a common area.

Christmas

Christmas is the second most important season in the Christian calendar as it celebrates Jesus' birth. From a Christian perspective this has multiple implications including:

- The fulfilment of ancient prophecy.

- God's humility in being born in a stable to an unwed mother.

- God's amazing love for people demonstrated by His stepping down from heaven and becoming human.

In terms of Christmas, in care homes and respite centres there are three primary options: decorations, church services and Carols by Candlelight.

Carols by Candlelight

Carols by Candlelight evenings have a strong tradition; however, this tradition has a significant dichotomy. Christian Carols by Candlelight feature carol singing interspersed with lessons (Christmas Bible readings). As such the focus is overtly Christian.

By contrast, secular Carols by Candlelight (such as those broadcast on TV) are more about Santa, Rudolf and entertainment. The challenge in care homes and dementia settings is that many people (even those who don't have strong Christian affiliation) expect 'proper' carols whereas their families often expect a Santa-centric approach. As such there's value in a hybrid option, with

Carols by Candlelight events including a mixture of Christian and secular components.

In terms of practicalities here are some thoughts to consider:

- In areas with a warm climate consider holding Carols by Candlelight outside (e.g. in a care home car park) as this provides enough space for both residents and families to attend.[11]

- A BBQ and ice cream on a stick are easy food options for a Southern Hemisphere Christmas. In the Northern Hemisphere mince pies and mulled wine are good cool weather options.

- Electric candles are always appreciated (not to mention that they're safer and less messy than wax candles).

- Having a printed programme with the carol or song words printed out makes it easier for everyone to sing. This has the added benefit of providing a great gift for people to take home with them at the end.

- Consider collaborating with a local church that may be able to provide a choir or a musician.

Further resources

Jesus Loves Me by Ben Boland and Dana Gruben (HammondCare, Sydney 2020).

---

11 As Australia has Christmas in summer, snow is never a problem, but outdoors in places blessed with white Christmases may find a car park less than ideal.

Joy to the World, by Ben Boland and Dana Gruben (HammondCare, 2020).

Messy Christmas: Three complete sessions and a treasure trove of craft ideas for Advent, Christmas and Epiphany, by Lucy Moore and Jane Leadbetter (IVP Books, 2012).

Messy Easter: Three complete sessions and a treasure trove of ideas for Lent, Holy Week and Easter, by Jane Leadbetter (BRF, 2014).

7

Discipleship

'Do older people and people living with dementia need to grow in their faith?' After all, if someone is already saved, can we not simply entrust them to God?

Scripture is clear that *all* Christians need to grow in their faith![1] However, different seasons of life bring different challenges. Generally speaking, there can be two interlocking spiritual challenges for older people and people living with dementia: loneliness and ill health.

> 'You whom I have upheld since your birth,
>   and have carried since you were born.
> Even to your old age and grey hairs
>   I am he, I am he who will sustain you.
> I have made you and I will carry you;
>   I will sustain you and I will rescue you.'
>   —Isaiah 46:3-4

---

1   For example: 1 Corinthians 3:1-3; Hebrews 5:12-14; 1 Peter 2:2-3, 3:18.

As we grow older, we often lose many relationships due to death and health issues. Additionally, it can become harder to make new friends because the pool of people we meet shrinks and health issues can impact communication (e.g. hearing loss) and opportunities to make new friends (e.g. no longer driving). Thus, loneliness is common among older people. For some Christians, this challenge is exacerbated by challenges around attending church (e.g. transport, seating, and continence).

Church is a great blessing, both relationally and spiritually. Growing older, however, can make it incredibly hard to attend, let alone be involved in, church. The loss of a driving licence, building design issues (e.g. lack of ramps, appropriate toilets and seating), continence and cognition problems can all conspire to make engagement in church nigh impossible. These 'practical issues' can be compounded because many churches 'focus on the young'. If all this was not enough, clergy turnover makes it very easy for an older person to be forgotten.

Yet the religion that God accepts, is to care for widows (James 1). Dare I write that 'the religion that God accepts', both generally and in terms of discipleship, starts with our three Ps: Prayer, Presence and Pastoral care?[2] We need to be praying with older people, we need to be present with older people and we need to provide pastoral care to older people. We need to do the same for people living with dementia.

---

2 See the earlier chapter 'Christian Love in the Context of Older People and People Living with Dementia' (p. 15, 23).

Discipleship starts with the Ps, but it also includes helping older people and people living with dementia to grow in their relationship with God. The challenge here is that no two older people are identical.

Let me introduce you to Mary and Martha, two real clergy widows who were dying. Mary spent hours each day using commentaries to compare the different Gospels. Martha struggled with the fear of dying (not death itself) and used hymns to encourage herself in her faith. Both were godly Christians, both were clergy widows and both were dying, but their discipleship needs were vastly different. The point here is that just like younger people, all older people are different and have different needs. The good news is that practising the three Ps allows you to know the individual in terms of their personality and their faith journey.

Another good practice is to make a habit of asking 'May I pray with you?' This empowers people by giving them control, something that's often elusive in the face of the challenges of getting older.[3] I also ask what they want to pray about. Often, I expect older people to ask for healing, mobility or pain management. Instead, they typically ask for prayers for a child, grandchild or great-grandchild who is about to sit exams, has just lost their boyfriend or girlfriend, or is looking for work. Asking what people want prayer for is a good precaution against the danger of making assumptions.[4]

---

3 A great examination of living with frailty can be found in Chapter 2 of *The Final Lap*, by John Wyatt (Leyland: 10Publishing, 2023).

4 Please read *My Body Is Not a Prayer Request: Disability Justice in the*

We can also assist with communication. Listening skills such as silence,[5] humour and meeting a person where they are[6] can overcome some of the common communication difficulties faced by some older people.[7] However, we also need to be aware that health issues can have other effects. For example, Christians tend to be 'people of the Book' and books.[8] Electronic devices mean many people can now access Scripture, sermons and other Christian content at the touch of a button. However, not all older people are tech-savvy and some have lost their ability to read.

For example, many older people can no longer access (or easily access) text because:

- Arthritic fingers struggle to turn pages, especially smooth, thin pages such as those found in most Bibles.

- A person with macular degeneration typically cannot see the middle of a projector screen clearly.

- Vision impairment means people need large print, yet large print typically means heavier books, which require more strength.

Church, Amy Kenny (Brazos Press, 2022).

5   Silence is powerful as it gives the other person space to speak and often draws out emotions. It also stops us from saying something that could be unhelpful, like Job's friends (Job 2:13).

6   For example, you may want to keep discussing Jesus' resurrection, but the person wants to reminisce about their garden – so reminisce!

7   There are numerous resources on listening skills and I highly recommend the *Clinical Pastoral Education* courses. Use Google to find one near you.

8   Commentaries, biographies of faith, Prayer Books – even books like this!

> Early on in my time as a chaplain, I rejoiced when I was able to give Alex a Bible as he had lost his own. A week later, in tears, I filled out an incident report. I had given Alex a Bible about the size and style of a traditional pew Bible. While reading it in his wheelchair, he fell asleep, and as it fell the corner of the cover gave him a significant skin tear on his thigh.

There are tips and tricks to help people overcome health issues that negatively impact their ability to read:

1. Devices

Not all older people are technophobic. Indeed, living with dementia doesn't mean a person can't learn to use modern devices.[9]

There are a range of devices designed specifically for people living with sensory loss or dementia (e.g. machines that magnify an image or text, easy-to-use phones and music players).

A cheap upgrade to a CD player for people who are vision impaired is to stick Velcro dots onto the buttons.

2. Large print literature

While we desperately need more, there are some large print, lightweight paper resources available.

---

9 *A person living with dementia learning to navigate an iPad: a case study*, Ingebrand, E., Samuelsson, C., & Hydén, L.-C. (2022). *Disability and Rehabilitation: Assistive Technology, 17*(5), 570–579. https://doi.org/10.1080/17483107.2020.1800117

One of my residents had a friend take a blade to the spine of a paperback Bible and cut it into sections. He then rebound each section individually making each one a volume of a manageable size.

3. Reading

Consider reading with older people. This can be done in person, over the phone or as part of a Bible reading group.

Further resources

Faith for Life Suite (https://www.hammond.com.au/shop/faith-for-life).

Faith in Later life (https://faithinlaterlife.org/).

The Touching Grace store (https://www.alzheimersministry.org/ministryaids.html).

Devotions for older people and people living with dementia.[10]

Bible Reflections for Older People, (Bible Reading Fellowship) https://www.brfonline.org.uk/collections/bible-reflections-for-older-people.

Heroes of the Bible: 30 Undated Devotions, Remaining Faithful Through Your Later Years, by Rodger Hitchings (10Publishing, 2015).

We are... Christian devotionals to share with a loved one living with dementia, by Tina English (https://www.embracingage.org.uk/).

---

10 I've also written devotions covering Luke, Acts and Philippians and am happy to share them. Please find me via LinkedIn.

8

Practical Tips

This chapter isn't strictly about Christian care for older people and people living with dementia. Instead, it covers some practical considerations about how to function most effectively within a care home and dementia pastoral context. So, if you're familiar with this context please just skim or even skip this chapter, but if you're new to visiting care homes or people living with dementia you'll hopefully get lots out of it.

Safety

We all know safety is everyone's priority. However, there are some significant safety issues that are not self-evident in the context of older people and dementia.

1. Please don't catch people who are falling! I realise this is extremely counterintuitive, but it's critical. The problem with trying to catch an older person isn't simply that you may hurt yourself, but that you're likely to seriously hurt the older person. Specifically, skin tears are extremely painful and slow to heal, much more so than broken bones.

2. Food and drink are dangerous! Specifically, many older people have swallowing issues and giving them the wrong food or drink could kill them.[1]

3. As many older people have serious health issues, minimising the chance of infection is crucial. From a ministry perspective the implications include prioritising hand hygiene and not visiting if we have symptoms of anything contagious.

4. While I'm aware there's a diversity of passionate views about vaccination, personally I believe in the value of having vaccinations, not primarily for my own health but as a way of loving people whose health is worse than mine. If you're vaccine-hesitant on health grounds, consider the impact to Timothy's health when he was circumcised for ministry purposes (Acts 16).

Oxygen concentrators

It's not uncommon for older people to use oxygen. In a care home setting this is typically supplied either via a bottle or an oxygen concentrator. Two pastoral challenges arise when someone is on oxygen. The first is being aware that they may be short of breath, and may therefore find talking difficult. The second challenge is specific to oxygen concentrators (see Figure 5) and is invisible.

Specifically, oxygen concentrators extract oxygen from the air. Therefore, particularly in a room with closed

---

1   For more on this topic please see the chapter 'Communion: Theology and Practice,' p. 109.

windows and doors, the oxygen level in the room can drop. Not to a point of being dangerous but certainly to a point where a visitor can become drowsy and start yawning. Thus, when visiting a person who is using an oxygen concentrator, consider asking whether you can open a window or leave the door open.

Visitors should avoid wearing, and using, strong fragrances (e.g. perfume and essential oils) around people who are using oxygen concentrators.[2]

Figure 5:
Oxygen Concentrator

Suicide

Talking about suicide isn't easy; however it's not uncommon for older people to want to die, or to plan and actually commit suicide. This is particularly true of older men.

It's common for older people to speak about struggling with meaninglessness, pain and fear. They may also be living with clinical depression, which is particularly common among people living with dementia. For some this is a form of venting, while others may be actively planning to end their lives. People providing pastoral care to older adults and people living with dementia need to be equipped to deal with both venting and suicidal ideation. Thankfully there are some great short training resources

---

2   *Spiritual Care for People Living with Dementia using Multisensory Interventions*, Richard Behers (Jessica Kingsley Publishers, 2018), p. 101.

> Modern church culture expects and encourages people to join together in worshipping God with praise and adoration, irrespective of the trauma they're experiencing.
>
> Certainly, there are many Psalms of praise and adoration, but there are more Psalms of lament.
>
> As such, should we not expect and encourage each other to join together in worshipping God 'in lament'?

available on mental health. I recommend the Mental Health First Aid short course[3] for generic understanding, and the Sanctuary Mental Health resources[4] for a specifically Christian understanding.

Until you can gain more training in this area, my summary is:

1. Mental health issues are real and affect Christians.[5]

2. If you are concerned someone may be suicidal, it's best practice to ask them directly e.g. 'You're sounding really down. Are you thinking about suicide?' If they answer, 'yes' then you need to ask 'Do you have a plan?'[6]

3. If the person has a suicide plan or you suspect they have a plan you need to seek professional assistance urgently. This may require notifying a

---

3   https://mhfa.com.au/.

4   https://www.sanctuarymentalhealth.org/.

5   Again, if you want to know more I recommend Sanctuary Mental Health, https://sanctuarymentalhealth.org/uk/.

6   Contrary to the common myth, raising the question of suicide doesn't put the idea in someone's head. It's likely to be there already!

professional against the wishes of the person.[7] In such a situation it's best to explain you need to get professional help for the person contemplating self-harm and ask for permission, but if permission isn't given you still need to notify a professional

> If a person is expressing a desire to kill themselves it's not appropriate to argue with them, 'tell the person off,' or give a biblical exposition on the evil of suicide!

immediately. For example, in a hospital or care home notify a nurse; in a community setting call a mental health hotline, hospital mental health unit or ambulance. As specifics will vary across jurisdictions, I recommend working out who to call in your context before you start pastoral ministry, as you don't want to be researching during a crisis.

4. Additionally, without endangering yourself, you need to prevent them from acting on their plan. Typically, this will simply mean staying with the person until the professionals arrive. I repeat, however, do *not* endanger yourself!

5. Even if a person says they're suicidal but they don't have a plan, professional help is still required and should be sought immediately.

---

7 For this reason, when people ask me about confidentiality I explain I'll keep a confidence with two exceptions – child abuse and a person at risk of harm.

After suicide

Sadly, despite increasing awareness, a large number of people die by suicide each year. You may therefore be faced with the aftermath of suicide both in your general life and in your ministry with older adults. This will probably include facing people's shock, anger and grief.

Such trauma calls for presence and listening from you, so you will require significant self-care and support. Additionally, it's important to remember that caring for people who have been touched by suicide is a risk factor for suicide – so don't neglect your self-care!

The following relates to grief generally but it's particularly important when grief is complex, as is the case after suicide.

Here are some applied biblical principles related to caring for the bereaved.

1. Loss and grief are always hard and often traumatic. They're directly linked to the Fall. Importantly grief, which often manifests in tears and anger, is good. Scripture tells us God grieves (e.g. Genesis 6 and Isaiah 63), and that Jesus wept at Lazarus' home, despite knowing that Lazarus would be alive again later that day (John 11).

2. Lamenting is a bold and biblical response to grief (e.g. Psalm 13, Psalm 22 and Lamentations). Lament can and should be 'robust'. In Psalm 13 David literally throws God's words back at Him. Practically, we need to remember our job isn't to

defend God. Instead, our role may be to join in the lament![8]

3. Silent presence is good. Job's friends did well when they sat silently for seven days and nights (Job 2). The problems started when they spoke. How often do we struggle to silently sit and grieve for seven minutes? If you're not sure what to say, say nothing. When you speak, the general rule is to start by expressing your sorrow at their loss.[9] If you do nothing other than offer your silence and share their sorrow you've done well.

Elder abuse

Thankfully domestic abuse and child abuse are no longer hidden topics. Sadly however, many people don't know about elder abuse.[10] Here is a summary:

1. Elder abuse is common in both society and the church.

2. The most common form of elder abuse is financial; however sexual, physical and psychological abuse all occur.

3. The most common abuser is a family member.

---

8 Romans 12.

9 Romans 12:15.

10 Language here is again problematic for three reasons. Firstly, the term 'elder' is considered ageist by many people today. Secondly, for many first nations people 'Elder' refers to community leaders. Thirdly, some Churches use the term 'Elder' as a church position. However, *Elder Abuse* is a recognised term for the abuse of older people!

4. Providing support for older people and their carers reduces the risk of elder abuse. As such, the church can play a powerful preventative role simply by engaging with older people and their caregivers.

5. There's evidence that COVID-19 saw an increase in elder abuse.[11]

Debriefing

Pastoral care can be invigorating, exciting and amazing, both generally and specifically in the context of ministry with older adults and people living with dementia. In my experience it's typically also exhausting, challenging and perplexing. As such, debriefing is often critically important.[12]

I currently meet with a retired minister most weeks as a chance to debrief and pray. Additionally, I sometimes debrief with other chaplains and see a counsellor. I've previously had seasons where I saw a professional pastoral supervisor,[13] which was also profoundly helpful. Such practices have supported, empowered and enriched both my pastoral work and my life more generally.

---

11 'Elder Abuse in the COVID-19 era based on calls to the National Center on Elder Abuse resource line', Weissberger, G. H., Lim, A. C., Mosqueda, L., Schoen, J., Axelrod, J., Nguyen, A. L., Wilber, K. H., Esquivel, R. S., & Han, S. D. (2022)., *BMC Geriatrics*, *22*(1). https://doi.org/10.1186/s12877-022-03385-w.

12 Debriefing is the process of talking through memories and feelings and is particularly valuable after a challenging event or encounter.

13 A pastoral supervisor is a person who has qualifications in helping people in pastoral ministry reflect on their practice. The gold standard is for everyone in ministry to have a pastoral supervisor.

How, and with whom, you debrief is a personal decision. It often takes time, effort, and trial and error to find the right person/s. Additionally the person/s will likely change over time. The following are some suggestions to help you find the right people to support your pastoral ministry:

1. Not your boss. No matter how wonderful they are, your boss should not be the only, or even the primary person you debrief with, for the following reasons: a) They may well be caught up with the same issue; b) They're likely to be busy and debriefing requires space and time; c) They may be the challenge you need to debrief about; d) They have HR responsibilities around your performance.

2. Not your spouse. It's best not to use your spouse as your primary source of debriefing because they're probably not the most qualified, they may struggle to be objective and it's not fair to overburden them.

3. Confidentiality is crucial. Effective debriefing needs total confidentiality. As such the person must be able to keep both your feelings and experiences, and the feelings and experiences of the people you're caring for, confidential. The exceptions to this are child abuse[14] and a person at risk of harm, the two circumstances where no one should maintain confidentiality. The example

---

14 As an older person's chaplain, I regularly deal with allegations of child abuse, which most often date back to an older person's childhood.

I typically use is: If you say your husband or the boss is a jerk it stays confidential. If you say I am going to hit my husband or the boss it does not remain confidential. In my experience the risk of harm is typically self-harm or suicide.

4. Faith. I prefer to debrief with a Christian because I want them to be praying for me and because they understand some of the challenges and jargon specific to Christianity.

5. Gender. I've greatly benefited from being able to debrief with people of both genders. However, as debriefing is emotionally intimate, when I'm debriefing with a woman, I intentionally practise strategies to guard against both adultery and the perception of adultery. Overall, having a diverse team of people to talk to is ideal.

Dress code

I can't tell you anything about fashion but here are three principles to consider when dressing for pastoral care work with older adults and people living with dementia.

First, if you're young, you'll find it helpful to dress more formally. When I started in chaplaincy at twenty-nine (yes, twenty-nine is either very young or very old depending on your current age!) I always wore a smart shirt and tie. Non-casual clothing is also ideal if you're running a church service or preaching.

Second, consider modesty[15] (yes gents, this applies to you too), particularly as engaging at people's head height requires a lot of bending over and crouching. The fact that people are older doesn't make them asexual. Furthermore, a lack of modesty can be offensive in some cultures.

Third, consider wearing something bright for three reasons:

1. It can help people living with dementia or vision impairment.

2. It provides a talking point or ice-breaker.

3. It makes you more memorable.

Humour

Humour is a powerful tool; indeed, some older people have a very dark sense of humour. There's a significant difference between laughing at ourselves and laughing at another person. Don't make a joke at the expense of an older person or a person living with dementia. However, you can certainly use many self-deprecating jokes. Laughter is good medicine and it helps to humanise you. For example, my standard response to a person asking, 'How are you?' is 'Still ugly but that's not going to change!' It typically gets a laugh.

---

15 What modesty looks like is highly variable across cultures, so it's critical to work within your specific context..

Further resources

Sanctuary Mental Health Ministries, https://sanctuarymentalhealth.org/.

Guarding against Elder Abuse in Church, by Ben Boland (Eternity, 2018), https://www.eternitynews.com.au/opinion/guarding-against-elder-abuse-in-church/.

Six signs of Elder Abuse and how you can help, by Ben Boland (Eternity, 2022) https://www.eternitynews.com.au/australia/six-signs-of-elder-abuse-and-how-you-can-help/.

There are numerous government websites where you can learn about elder abuse.[16]

---

16 I've not included links as different jurisdictions will have different websites and websites change.

9

Ministry with the Silent

Many older people are silent or, more technically, non-verbal which can make ministering to them challenging. My hope is that this chapter might encourage and equip you to minster well in this context.

Perhaps the best starting point is to note that people can be silent for a range of reasons, and the first rule is to always assume a person can understand you. I remember listening to a son say across his low-verbal[1] mother's bed 'if mum was a dog we would put her down'. The look on her face was terrible. The basic rule is to never say something in front of a person you wouldn't say if they were verbal.

However, not saying anything wrong is insufficient. As Christians we want to share Jesus' love with all people including those who are non-verbal. Thankfully there are several ways we can do so and a number of these have already been raised in the previous chapters. For example, offering Prayer, our Presence and Pastoral Care is crucial for the care of all.

---

1   She rarely spoke.

The second rule of ministry to people who are verbally challenged isn't to simply assume they can understand, but to also assume they're intelligent! Too often people in wheelchairs and those who are non-verbal are treated as if they're stupid. Neither using a wheelchair nor being silent has any link with a lack of intelligence or understanding. On the contrary, Proverbs 17:28 actually equates silence with intelligence:

> Even a fool who keeps silent is considered wise;
> when he closes his lips, he is deemed intelligent. (ESV)

Many people who have limited ability to speak are highly intelligent and find not being able to communicate effectively incredibly frustrating. Take a moment to consider the chain of functions required for the simplest verbal exchange. If one link is worn or broken the exchange will suffer.

Words are spoken; the ear receives the vibrations; the message of the vibrations is transmitted to the brain; the brain deciphers the vibrations to words; the brain processes the meaning of the words; a response is generated; the response is coded into words; words are sent to the mouth and throat words are articulated as intelligible sounds.[2]

For some people the challenge isn't that the links are broken but that the links are 'weak'. Giving people the time to process and respond is crucial. There's a reason why finishing another person's sentences is considered rude. Equally, not travelling at a conversational speed

---

2   Actually, this is a simplified version of the complexity of verbal exchange.

suitable to the person you're conversing with stops it being a conversation. For example, if I am talking with someone for whom English is a new language, I deliberately slow down my speech. Whereas it's important to note that some non-verbal people can process at incredibly high speeds, their challenge is simply responding verbally. As such they may enjoy simply listening to you talk as listening can bring your world to them.

Even if a person can't speak, there are a number of other ways they can communicate e.g. sign language, small white boards, point sheets, body language and touch. Often, the problem doesn't lie with the person who is non-verbal but with the verbal person who is trying to keep up or understand. As such, it's important to get to know the non-verbal person and to become fluent in their preferred communication method.

For example, Zoë was a French lady I had the privilege of visiting. When I first met her, she would normally use English so communication was easy. As her dementia progressed I could ask her to use English which usually worked. When her knowledge of English deteriorated further, I could use my phone to play French music or communicate with simple sentences. Later she stopped speaking completely. So, we communicated through gestures. When I saw her, I would smile broadly and bow which would get a laugh. I would then spend time just smiling 'at' her.

Having covered the basics of general care and communication with people who find speech hard, it's worth considering Christian spiritual care in the context of people with limited verbal communication. At the risk of stating the obvious, people who struggle to, or cannot speak, can and do become Christians and grow in their faith. The question is simply how we communicate so we can understand them and they us. Some practical suggestions include:

- Prayer.

- Presence: just being with and facilitating a person being with others in a group setting can be profoundly powerful.

- Touch: holding someone's hand can be incredibly significant. Touch is a complicated topic (both with reference to infection control and potential for abuse) and will be dealt with in some detail in the following chapter. It's critical to ensure any touch requires prior consent.

- Music, video and audio material (e.g. audio Bible and podcasts).

- Church services and Bible studies.

None of these are unique to ministry with people who are non-verbal or low verbal, so be encouraged. You have the skills. Go and use them.

10

Boundaries

Many people who are drawn towards pastoral ministry, do so because they care – often deeply. Moreover, as Christians we know we're called to show sacrificial love. The 'problem' of care is that it's easy to become overwhelmed by people's needs. As a result, some people avoid pastoral care work because they're afraid it will overwhelm them.

The practical solution to both these responses is to establish effective boundaries. But are boundaries biblical?

Yes. Jesus' ministry regularly demonstrated boundaries. Jesus retreated to lonely places to pray, traversed a lake to get away from crowds and only had twelve disciples. He also regularly crossed both societal and cultural boundaries to care for outcasts: he touched lepers,[3] ate with sinners[4] and talked to the Samaritan woman at the well.[5]

---

3   Matthew 8; Luke 5.

4   Matthew 9:10-17; Mark 2:15-22; Luke 5:29-39.

5   John 4.

Inhibition and Sensory Loss

Early in my chaplaincy experience, when my children were small, they would sometimes come and visit the people in the care home.

One day, I passed two ladies in the corridor. About a metre past them I heard the following:

'Who's that?'

'It's the man with the terrible children.'

This cameo highlights three common challenges of ageing:

1. People can speak more loudly because of a hearing impediment.
2. People can lose their inhibitions, particularly those with some dementias.
3. People can become self-absorbed.

Together these factors can lead to people making comments that can be quite hurtful. However, it's worth remembering there's typically no desire to offend or attack behind the comments.

Sadly, today many older people and those living with dementia are treated as outcasts. As we've seen, we have a responsibility to love *all* people and to cross sociocultural divides with the love of Jesus.

Equally, as older people and people living with dementia are human, we need boundaries. To use a rural analogy, some sheep never touch even the flimsiest fences.[6] Other sheep require incredibly robust fences. The same is true

---

6   Isaiah 53 teaches we're all like sheep.

of personal relationships. Some people never come near our boundaries; others regularly push against them.

Four basic boundaries

When visiting care homes, I find it helpful to set out four basic boundaries: topic, abuse, length and self-care.

Topic

As a chaplain I regularly listen to people talk about a diverse range of topics. There are however a few topics I'm not comfortable discussing or even listening to someone else talk about.

Some of these are generic; for example, I don't need to hear details of a person's sexual fantasies. Other topics are specific to me and generally relate to traumas I've faced and still have scar tissue from. Irrespective of whether a person wants to talk about such topics, I'll gently but clearly explain I'm not comfortable (and perhaps offer to refer them).[7] If they continue to speak about these topics, I'll excuse myself.

Abuse

Another boundary relates to people who are verbally abusive.[8] Older people and people living with dementia are no more or less abusive than other people. Verbal

---

7 I regularly refer people to counsellors, psychologists and other ministry professionals.

8 The topic of verbal abuse brings with it the question of swearing/foul language. While I endeavour not to use such language, I also don't react when people use language I don't use. To quote a prison chaplain I once knew: 'swearing is just punctuation' for many people.

abuse is the most common type, but all other forms (i.e. sexual, physical, emotional, and psychological) can and do occur.

The compounding challenge of advancing years and cognitive decline can impact disinhibition and make it difficult for older people and people living with dementia to change their inappropriate behaviour. For example, Betty had spent much of her life living in South Africa during the time of apartheid and she was used to having servants. In the dining room or lounge she would call out 'Help please' and if the person who answered was blessed with significant melanin she would then say, 'White help please'. Clearly such behaviour is biblically abhorrent. If the person can be reasoned with, it's appropriate to gently but clearly explain to them that their behaviour is wrong.

Language

While some people have used swearing as a form of punctuation throughout their lives, and thus continue to swear as they age, others who've never been heard to swear, suddenly manifest a 'new' vocabulary.

There are typically two medical factors related to dementia behind such a change. The first is loss of inhibition where a person might have thought, but not uttered, particular words.

The second relates to language learning and storage. When a child is learning a language, 'special' words are stored in a different part of the brain to 'normal' words. Thus, when a person loses either normal words or the pathway to normal words due to dementia, they may retain and use 'special' words.

If the person can't be reasoned with, or is simply unwilling to cease being abusive, then boundaries are the answer.

Five possible boundaries, in no particular order, are:

1. Spatial – restricting visiting in a common or public area.

2. Responsive – 'If you say ... again I'll have to leave'.

3. Team – visiting in a pair or group.

4. Referral – asking someone else to provide pastoral care for a particular individual.

5. Chronological – limiting the length or frequency of an interaction.

Length

Limiting the length of a visit deserves further explanation as it's a common challenge in pastoral ministry. Here are some strategies to employ:

- I start the visit with a clear expectation such as 'Betty, I can only stay for ... minutes today'.

- Place the visit against another appointment or a mealtime. For example, 'I have a haircut at 11:00' or 'I don't want to interfere with your lunch'.

- Set an alarm on my phone. 'Sorry James, my alarm has just gone. I need to go.'

- Organise for someone to come and 'rescue' me physically or via phone at an arranged time.

Self-Care

Last, but by no means least, is the topic of self-care. This relies on the practice of boundaries. There are books covering this significant topic. I primarily struggle with self-care because my theology is wrong or, at least, it's not applied. The following are three biblical truths I need to remember:

- God is all powerful – He chooses to minister with and through me but doesn't need me.

- God created humans as limited beings, so I can't do everything that needs doing (and I shouldn't try).

- Rest, generally, and Sabbath rest, specifically, are essential – and biblical.

Further resources

Boundaries: When to Say Yes, How To Say No To Take Control Of Your Life, by Henry Cloud and John Townsend (HarperCollins, 2006).

11

End-of-Life Care

In life, and in our ministry with older people and people living with dementia, we're always in the midst of death. Dementia is the biggest killer of women in Australia and much of the Western world, and the average stay in an Australian care home is under two years. Therefore, ministry to older people and people living with dementia[1] is palliative[2] ministry.

To engage with this reality effectively, we need to first examine a myth or, perhaps more accurately, an emotional statement of grief: 'I lost mum twice: Once to dementia, once to death'. Dementia can often change people, and their ability to relate, at a terrifying speed. Not being recognised is certainly highly traumatic. However, although rapid change and trauma are challenging and require deep grieving, neither constitute death. To describe someone living with dementia as 'dead' or a 'lifeless, empty shell' is highly offensive and contributes to

---

1   Dementia is terminal.

2   Palliative care isn't limited to when a person is actively dying but refers to care where the focus is quality of life rather than cure.

Dying Definitions

Advanced Care Directive: A document outlining what care a person does or doesn't want to receive. This is a crucial document not simply for older people but for everyone. Much like a will, every adult should have one and regularly update it. On a practical note, advanced care directives should be discussed with your loved ones.

NFR: Not For Resuscitation, in other words, don't perform CPR (Cardiopulmonary resuscitation).

Palliative Care: Care focused on quality of life rather than its continuation. Please note that palliative care isn't simply not performing interventions. It's active! Additionally, it's not uncommon for palliative care to last for years.

Actively Dying: From the moment we're conceived we're all dying. Active dying is the final stage of the dying process. Typically, this process takes a few days as the body shuts down. Common symptoms include cold hands (as the heart slows), breathing changes (e.g. 'gappy' breathing) and low, or no, consciousness.

the view that euthanasia is the logical and compassionate 'cure' for dementia.

Scripture is clear: all people bear God's image and are immutably valuable irrespective of their race, age, and function. Additionally, as people generally, and Christians specifically, we're called to love our neighbours as ourselves and older people in particular.

How do we provide end-of-life care for older people and those living with dementia? We start with the three

Ps: Prayer, Presence and Pastoral care. Our relationship with the older person or person living with dementia helps us consider who they are and their general wishes, as well as their relationship with Jesus.

It's important to pause here to reflect on the nature of a Christian's relationship with Jesus and whether memory loss affects that relationship.

Some Christians fear they may lose their salvation if they forget Jesus. Biblically, the answer to this fear is beautifully expressed in the title of John Swinton's book *Dementia: Living in the Memories of God*.

Theologically, we know we're saved by Christ alone and not by any contribution of our own either pre- or post-conversion. If God saved us when we were 'dead in our transgressions,'[3] we can rest assured He holds onto us even when we forget Him. If we're honest, we all forget God every day – whether we're living with dementia or not!

Additionally, as previously detailed, God can and does bring people into relationship with Him in the midst of dementia.

Finally, let me quote the old saying 'between the saddle and the ground, salvation can be found', which reminds us that salvation can occur a split second before death.

Let me tell you about Alf. When I met Alf, a retired minister, his advanced dementia meant he was living in a secure dementia unit. He was almost non-verbal and spent most of his waking hours in apparent agitation walking up and down the corridor. From his life history, I knew of Alf's faith, despite his inability to articulate it.

---

3 Ephesians 2.

Therefore, as part of caring for him, I tried walking with him, reading the Bible with him and singing hymns with him… with minimal success in reducing his agitation. One day, I offered to pray for him and I prayed a best-practice dementia prayer (short and concrete). Then Alf, who rarely spoke five words a day, started to pray. His prayer had depth beyond my best prayer on my best day. Alf could no longer easily speak to me and other people, but he could certainly speak to his Lord and God!

Of course, not everyone has the depth of relationship with Jesus that I saw manifested in Alf, so in preparing to care for people who are dying, we must be able to share the good news of Jesus quickly, gently and clearly.

For example, I hadn't previously met Ruth when a nurse asked me to visit her. Ruth was dying (the nurse was Roman Catholic, and I think wanted me to give Ruth the last rites). I knocked on Ruth's door and said, 'My name's Ben. I'm the chaplain. Can I please come in?' She replied, 'Yes. How can I be right with God?' No small talk, no lead up, literally just 'How can I be right with God?' I simply explained that Jesus loved her, had died for her and she needed to trust Him. We then prayed a very short prayer. She dozed off minutes later and died without regaining consciousness. I look forward to dancing with her in eternity. (Hopefully my

Practice Makes Perfect

If you're not confident you can share Jesus' love in under two minutes, my recommendation is to practise.

Specifically, I suggest you practise when you're sitting on the toilet. Not only will this not cost you much time, but it's also a private space.

new body is less likely to step on my partner's toes than this one!)

Ruth's story highlights the importance of not simply practising the three Ps but being able to share the good news of a relationship with Jesus. Interestingly, the ability to share Jesus' love clearly and simply can be eroded by theology. I've met numerous Christians who've sat under superb theological teaching. However, in wrestling with the depths of theology, they cannot explain Christ crucified. I'm a huge fan of theology and wrestling with the deep things of God, but we must always be able to respond unpretentiously and transparently using everyday language.

We need to express the gospel of Jesus simply and clearly not just for the sake of people like Ruth who didn't know Jesus, nor for people such as Alf whose faith towers over mine, but to remind ourselves of Jesus' power! So, in two short sentences or less, can you explain your faith? If not, you need to learn and practise until you can. Yes, there are excellent resources and tools available, but we also need to be able to give an answer without prior notice.

Having emphasised the importance of always being ready 'without a plan', I also want to encourage you to plan. Typically, death from old age or dementia is not rapid, which means there's time to plan how you provide pastoral care. Here are some tips:

Prayer

- Pray before you visit, when you're with the person and after the visit.

- Ask the person if you can pray with them and what they would like prayed for.[4]

- Aim for short and concrete prayers when you're with the person. For example:

  - God, lead us in your ways. Amen.

  - Father, draw Frank to yourself. Amen.

  - Lord, we know you're with June. We ask that she may feel your presence. Amen.

- Don't be afraid to ask God to take someone to be with Him. When I pray this aloud, I obviously ask permission from the person or next of kin first.

- If I'm unsure of a person's relationship with God I typically pray 'draw [person's name] to Yourself'.

- I'm often asked to pray for the recently departed. Biblically, there are examples of prayers for the deceased. Typically, these are prayers for immediate resurrection, of which the resurrection of Lazarus is probably the best remembered.[5] Though I've considered praying such a prayer with older people, I've hesitated because many older Christians resonate with Paul (Phil. 1:23) and are rightly passionate for eternity with Jesus.

- However, I often pray with the deceased either alone or in the presence of family, friends and staff.

---

4   *My Body Is Not a Prayer Request: Disability Justice in the Church*, Amy Kenny (Brazos Press, 2022).

5   Others include 1 Kings 17:17-24; 2 Kings 4:18-37; Luke 7:11-17, 8:49-56; Acts 9:36-42, 20:7-12.

I offer a prayer of thanks for the person's life, give thanks for God's love and request that the bereaved may know and experience God's love, peace, hope and even joy in the midst of their tears.

Listening

- Yes, you need to listen but never forget that people can hear long after they cease to respond. As such, continue to use words, even if the person is non-responsive. We simply don't know how much they can hear. Again, never say anything you wouldn't say if you expected them to speak.

Scripture

- Learn some key Bible passages, both the reference (so you can read it from your phone) and as stories. Tell the story in your own words; you don't need to be word perfect.

- Some basic texts are: 'the Lord is my shepherd' (Ps. 23), the Lord's Prayer (Matt. 6), the resurrection of Lazarus (John 11), 'in my Father's house' (John 14) and the thief on the cross (Luke 23).

- Read the Psalms with the person's name inserted (e.g. 'The Lord is [person's name] shepherd…')

- Ask the person what they would like to read! As a teen I visited an older lady from church who was dying in hospital. Because I had no idea what passage to read, I asked her. With some passion she said 'NOT the Psalms' as her family had been reading only Psalms with her, and she wanted something else. So, we read from some of Paul's letters.

- If you have a mental blank, pray for inspiration and ask Google to suggest Bible passages for the dying.

Music

- Learn some timeless hymns and be willing to sing them with the person. Singing with a dying person isn't an audition for a TV show, so your singing ability isn't relevant.

- Consider using your phone to play some Christian music.[6]

Touch

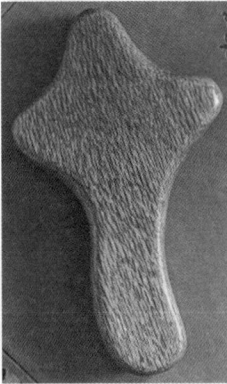

Figure 6:
A Holding Cross

- Use appropriate touch (e.g. let the person hold your hand if they wish).

- Get a 'holding cross' (see Figure 6). These are available online and are easy for a woodworker to make. They are not holy in and of themselves but fit nicely into the hand and some people benefit from a tactile reminder of Jesus' death.

---

6   If you plan to use your phone I suggest explaining what you are going to do so it doesn't look like you're checking your emails or playing games on it.

Family and friends

- Typically, when you're caring for a person who's dying, you're not just caring for them. Often, there are family, friends and staff to look after as well. Consider and care for them too.

Self-care

- Caring for the dying is draining. Just as Jesus took time to be alone to rest and to be with God, we also need to prioritise self-care.

- Boundaries are a core component of self-care.[7]

Caring is a significant component of love and love is never cheap. Remember:

- God designed us to love.

- God inspires us to love.

- God empowers us to love.

Further resources

Living in the Memories of God, by John Swinton (SCM Press, 2012).

Palliative Care, Ageing and Spirituality: A Guide for Older People, Carers and Families, by Elizabeth MacKinlay (Jessica Kingsley Publishers, 2012).

---

7   See the chapter on Boundaries (p. 81).

12

Voluntary Assisted Dying

Voluntary assisted dying (VAD) is a very emotive and important topic so it's important to define it clearly. The definition from *Remaining in Lament* is excellent:

What is Voluntary Assisted Dying?
Voluntary Assisted Dying (VAD) gives people who are suffering and dying, and who meet the eligibility criteria, the option of requesting medical assistance to end their lives.

This is different from other end-of-life processes such as the withdrawal of treatment by withholding or withdrawing overly burdensome medical treatment from a person because of medical futility or non-beneficial care; and relieving suffering through palliative care interventions that may unintentionally hasten a person's death. In Queensland, voluntary assisted dying is governed by the Voluntary Assisted Dying Act.

Voluntary: Consent, free from coercion, capacity.
Assisted: Access to substance to legally end life, and practitioner administration.

Dying: Intention is to end the life of the person.[1]

There are four points to highlight from this definition:

1. VAD means people choosing to end their own lives with medical assistance.

2. VAD legislation varies across jurisdictions, so please learn what the legislation is in yours.

3. Withdrawing or not giving treatment on the basis of quality of life isn't VAD. Indeed, I believe withdrawal or not starting treatment is a biblically robust option.

4. Treatment intended to help (e.g. pain relief), which unintentionally leads to death is also not VAD. Again, I believe such treatment is a biblically robust option.

It's also important to summarise what the Bible says in relation to VAD:

1. God created people in His image. Thus, human beings are immutably valuable.

2. God tells His people to not kill humans. While this primarily applies to killing other people, it also applies to oneself and to assisting someone else to kill themselves. As such, while some taking of life is biblically warranted,[2] for example capital punishment and war, even this killing isn't good (1 Chron. 22).

---

1   *Remaining in Lament and Hope: A Pastoral Response for a Voluntary Assisted Dying Pathway*, by UnitingCare (UnitingCare, 2022), p. 19.

2   There is a diversity of views on this among Christians.

3. The Bible is clear that, although we live in an incredibly broken world with unimaginable suffering, God is good and He's in control.

Therefore, I believe VAD is not biblical.

However, I don't expect people who don't know Jesus to adhere to teachings of the Bible. I also know Christians sin, and that includes me. So, I recommend strong caution before judging those who contemplate, request or use VAD.

It is our role to love people, particularly when we believe they've made bad decisions. Furthermore, depending on your jurisdiction, trying to convince people not to engage in VAD may be illegal.

Some Christians will choose to deal with VAD by simply not engaging with a person who's requested VAD. While I respect this decision, I think it better to continue to be with them and to love them.

> In my time as a chaplain, I've never seen a person die in physical agony. Indeed, outside of a traumatic incident such as a car accident, no one who's receiving medical care should be in agony.

Further resources

Remaining in Lament and Hope: A Pastoral Response for a Voluntary Assisted Dying Pathway, by UnitingCare (UnitingCare, 2022).

13

Church and Preaching

I'm passionate about both church services and preaching particularly with older congregations and people living with dementia. Yet I've left this chapter towards the end as not everyone involved in ministry to older people and people living with dementia conducts church services or preaches. Even if you don't exercise these ministries, please reflect on this chapter as the communication strategies are all highly applicable across pastoral ministry. As there are a plethora of great resources on conducting services and preaching generally, I'll confine myself to offering tips for leading services and preaching for older people and people living with dementia specifically.

Church

The following are some suggestions to help run an effective church service designed for older adults or people living with dementia.

- Mid-morning is the best time to conduct a church service (and any other event), as this is when the highest proportion of older adults and people living with dementia are most alert.

- Particularly for people living with dementia, style the service towards their early memories.

- Allow the congregation time to move their focus between segments. For example, allow the Bible reader to regain their seat before the sermon starts.

1915–1950s Church

People living with dementia often have strong childhood memories, and Sunday School was very popular in the early twentieth century. With this in mind, I researched church service styles and the most memorable songs from this period across the English-speaking world. These were my findings, and I use them when designing church services:

The most memorable songs are: 'Amazing Grace', 'Blessed Assurance', 'Count Your Blessings', 'Jesus Loves Me' and 'The Lord is My Shepherd'.

Unlike today, church services of the period were very similar across denominations. The basic liturgy was as follows:

- Welcome
- Confession and Absolution
- Creed
- Bible Readings
- Sermon
- Prayers
- The Blessing

Preaching

The complaint I hear most often about sermons is that they're too long. As a preacher I suspect sermons are long because, at best, we've learnt so much from the text we want to share it all; at worst, a long sermon is a mark of poor preparation. I've been guilty of both.

So, how long is too long? The best answer is: Preach for as long as you can keep the congregation engaged. For services in care homes and dementia-friendly settings the simpler answer is a maximum of five to ten minutes.[1]

Yes, it's hard to preach a good three-minute sermon, let alone a great one. In fact, it often takes longer to prepare a very short sermon than a 'normal' one. What's more, preaching to older congregations and people living with dementia presents some extra challenges. Specifically:

- Often older adults and people living with dementia are facing the hardest challenges of their lives.

- There are often 'cultural Christians'[2] who need to hear about Jesus' transforming love.

- The congregation is likely to include people from a range of church traditions and denominations.

---

1   Unless your congregation consists of university students who are used to fifty-minute monologues, most people are trained to a seven-minute attention span, i.e. the length between ad breaks on television. Moreover, every minute of TV has several hours of preparation by multiple experts behind it. Yes, my current favourite preacher's podcast sermons are over forty-five minutes long. But he's a better preacher than me!

2   People who identify as Christians, and who may have been in and around churches all their life, but don't have a relationship with Jesus.

- Both older age and dementia can often lead to shortened attention spans, which can make it harder for people to process information.

- Many older adults and people living with dementia cannot easily access Scripture[3] so church may be the only time, or a key time, they hear God's Word.

- There's strong support in the literature about preaching as a component of dementia.[4]

As such, it's clear that preaching in the context of older congregations and dementia-friendly church is both very challenging and incredibly important.

So how can we preach well in these contexts? Here are some basic principles:

- Pray. Preaching must be underpinned by prayer.

- Build relationships. Relationships are powerful. I strongly believe we have a God-ordained instruction to share Jesus' love. However, most people listen because of relationship.

- Dress well. Most older people remember wearing their 'Sunday best' to church, so smart[5] is generally best. I typically robe (wear a surplice and stole, see Figure 7), not because I'm more comfortable robing[6] but because, from the 1920s to the

---

3   See the chapter on Discipleship (p. 59).

4   *Pastoral Reflection: Effective Church for People Living with Dementia – Seven principles and a Proposed Service Guide*, by Ben Boland (Stimulus)

5   Not casual.

6   I've happily preached barefoot and wearing shorts and a T-shirt.

1950s, church leaders across denominations typically wore robes. Additionally, many churches still expect their clergy to robe. In particular, robing helps people living with memory loss to identify the context as church. This is particularly significant in care homes and respite centres where church is held in a multi-purpose room.

Figure 7:
Robed for
Church

- Even people living with quite advanced dementia can, and do, learn.

- God is more powerful than both ageing and dementia.

- Remember many in your congregation will be living with vision and hearing loss. So:

  - Speak slowly and clearly.

  - Use big gestures.

  - If you have facial hair, trim around your mouth to help lip reading.

  - If you can, encourage or arrange that people who are living with hearing or vision loss sit near the front.

  - If the space has a hearing loop use a microphone attached to the hearing loop and encourage people with hearing aids to tune in.

- Consider printing out the Bible passage so people can follow it and then take Scripture home. This also helps people with hearing loss to engage with the text.

- Your sermon should have only one point and a clear application to people's lives.[7]

- Care home and dementia-friendly preaching involves preaching to adults so, though always simple, it should never be simplistic.

- Stories, humour, repetition and questions are all powerful devices. However, remember some people living with dementia may have lost their inhibitions. So, expect rhetorical questions to be answered!

- Consider using multimedia: music, videos, objects and skits. I often perform a one-man skit of the passage.

- Some people argue communication with people living with dementia should focus on positives and that therefore, sermons should be focused on 'love, mercy and grace'.[8] Certainly some people living with dementia can get 'stuck' on something negative. However, Jesus' preaching included both powerful positives and honest negatives such as the reality of life without a relationship with God. I think William May puts it well:

---

7   I realise three points (or more) are common but the practical question is: By Wednesday how many points can the congregation remember?

8   *In a Strange Land… People with Dementia and the Local Church* by Malcolm Goldsmith (4M Publications, 2004), p. 192.

Our reluctance to question or challenge older people may subtly remove them from the human race. It pretends, in effect, that they are moral non-entities; it treats them condescendingly as though they were toys. We will take an important step towards re-entry into community with the aged when we are willing to attend to them seriously enough as moral beings to approve and reprove their behaviour.[9]

- Finally, remember that no plan survives 'contact with the enemy' or indeed with a beloved congregation. So, don't expect a service or sermon to go the way you planned – instead plan hard and roll with the punches.

Preaching, and particularly preaching to older people and people living with dementia, is especially challenging. However, be encouraged that preaching in this context improves over time.[10] Additionally, I'm confident God speaks even through the weakest of his preachers. My prayer is that this chapter is a seed, a starting point from which your preaching will grow.

Further resources

Celebrating the Seasons in Residential Care Homes: A service for every week of the year, by Lindsay Pelloquin and Jaye Keightley (The Paul Thomas Group, 2022).

---

9 William F. May, 'The Virtues and Vices of the Elderly', in Thomas R. Cole and Sally A. Gadow (eds), *What Does It Mean to Grow Old? Reflections from the Humanities* (Duke University Press, 1986), p. 43.

10 The great Australian preacher Chappo (John Chapman) said 'the first fifty years are the hardest'. He later amended this to a longer period as he got older!

Dementia-Friendly Worship: A Multifaith Handbook for Chaplains, Clergy and Faith Communities, by Lynda Everman and Don Wendorf (eds.) (Jessica Kingsley Publishers, 2019).

'Creating a Church Service to Facilitate Belonging for People Living with Dementia – Seven Principles and a Service Guide', by Ben Boland, *Stimulus: The New Zealand Journal of Christian Thought and Practice,* 32.1, 2025

14

Communion

THEOLOGY AND PRACTICE

Writing about Communion in a book designed for use across Christian denominations is challenging due to the diversity of theological positions and practices. This diversity is reflected in the names used (the Eucharist, Holy Communion and the Lord's Supper). Therefore, the first part of this chapter doesn't seek to propose or support a specific theology of Communion as much as to examine some key challenges Communion needs to consider. By contrast, the second section is more directive as it highlights some practical challenges and possible solutions for sharing Communion with older people and people living with dementia.

A theology of Communion for older people and people living with dementia

Despite the diversity of different theological positions within Christendom, Scripture clearly instructs Christians

> 'We need to move from a politics of inclusion to a theology of belonging.'
> —John Swinton
> Keynote address, 28th October 2019, 8th International Conference on Ageing and Spirituality Canberra

to celebrate Communion (e.g. Matt. 26, Luke 22 and 1 Cor. 10). However, in the context of older congregations and people living with dementia, there are two challenges: corporate and cognitive.

By corporate, I mean that the Passover, Last Supper and Communion as recorded in Scripture were corporate rather than individual events. Communion has been primarily celebrated as part of a church gathering rather than private sacrament. The problem is that simply getting to church can be a major obstacle for many older people and for people living with dementia. While taking Communion to people's homes is of value, I suggest this should be an option of last resort, as churches should not merely be *welcoming* but also *actively seeking to engage with* older people and people living with dementia.

A potentially more complicated theological challenge is the level of cognitive assent required for a person to partake in Communion. Biologically, the challenge is that cognition is fluid not only over the course of a lifespan but also over a twenty-four-hour period. As such, if a theological position requires a specific level of cognition, it also needs to recognise that a person's cognition is fluid.[1]

---

1   Variable cognition is one of the reasons I suggest church services for older people and people living with dementia occur in the morning as this is likely to be when they're at their best mentally.

Moreover, Christians must remember that faith is more than cognition so we mustn't fall into the modern Western cultural heresy of hyper-cognition.[2]

Additionally, I think it's important to examine what Scripture makes clear about Communion:

- All the people of Israel were commanded to celebrate Passover (Exod. 12), not just those with 'good' cognition.

- The Last Supper included Judas (who betrayed Jesus), Peter (who claimed he would never deny Christ), and the disciples who were squabbling over who would be greatest (Matt. 26, Mark 14, Luke 22 and John 13). As such, while the disciples' cognitive ability isn't in question, their thoughts were less than ideal.

- 1 Corinthians 11:17-34 certainly commands Christians to treat Communion very seriously:

  In the following directives I have no praise for you, for your meetings do more harm than good. In the first place, I hear that when you come together as a church, there are divisions among you, and to some extent I believe it. No doubt there have to be differences among you to show which of you have God's approval. So then, when you come together, it is not the Lord's Supper you eat, for when you are eating, some of you go ahead with your own private suppers. As a result, one person remains hungry and another gets drunk. Don't you

---

2   Hyper-cognition is the view that a person's value and personhood is found in the mind.

have homes to eat and drink in? Or do you despise the church of God by humiliating those who have nothing? What shall I say to you? Shall I praise you? Certainly not in this matter!

For I received from the Lord what I also passed on to you: The Lord Jesus, on the night He was betrayed, took bread, and when He had given thanks, He broke it and said, 'This is my body, which is for you; do this in remembrance of me.' In the same way, after supper He took the cup, saying, 'This cup is the new covenant in my blood; do this, whenever you drink it, in remembrance of me.' For whenever you eat this bread and drink this cup, you proclaim the Lord's death until he comes.

So then, whoever eats the bread or drinks the cup of the Lord in an unworthy manner will be guilty of sinning against the body and blood of the Lord. Everyone ought to examine themselves before they eat of the bread and drink from the cup. For those who eat and drink without discerning the body of Christ eat and drink judgement on themselves. That is why many among you are weak and sick, and a number of you have fallen asleep. But if we were more discerning with regard to ourselves, we would not come under such judegment. Nevertheless, when we are judged in this way by the Lord, we are being disciplined so that we will not be finally condemned with the world.

So then, my brothers and sisters, when you gather to eat, you should all eat together. Anyone who is hungry should eat something at home, so that when you meet together it may not result in judgement.

And when I come I will give further directions.

- Both the liturgy around Communion and the sensory impact of the bread and wine can be powerful 'memory triggers' that help people remember Jesus.

- Christians considering 'fencing'[3] Communion must wrestle with how to manage the commandment that all Christians celebrate Communion (Mark 14 and 1 Cor. 11).

- In churches where church discipline includes not offering Communion to those under discipline, not offering Communion to people living with cognitive challenges is problematic.

Overall, I think part of the reason Christians hold such a diversity of views about Communion is because the biblical instructions are quite limited.

My personal practice when celebrating Communion is to explain what Communion is and to invite anyone, irrespective of denomination, who 'knows Jesus as their Lord and saviour' to partake. I've often experienced people (particularly Catholics) who are not comfortable receiving Communion from someone outside their own denomination. I respect their point of view, and I typically touch base with them after the service to explain I'm not offended. But this is my position. Other greater minds than mine have strongly held divergent views.

---

3   Verbally or physically limiting people from celebrating Communion.

The practice of administering Communion to older people and people living with dementia

Celebrating Communion with older people and people living with dementia can present some critical challenges, critical because getting them wrong can kill. This may seem like hyperbole but allergies, choking and aspiration (getting food or drink in the lungs) are very real risks for many older people.

Celebrating Communion with older people and people living with dementia requires planning, and this starts with knowing the needs of those who want to partake.[4] For example, 'wine' options may need to include alcoholic wine,[5] non-alcoholic wine and wine that has been thickened. There are typically three levels of thickened fluid used for people with swallowing difficulties. The good news is that it's possible to purchase sealed cups of thickened juice or tins of powder to easily make up any level of thickened fluid (see Figure 8).

Figure 8:
Thickening Fluids

In terms of the 'bread', my recommendation is to use wafers.

---

4   Ideally this will mean communicating directly with the person who wants to take Communion, but dementia or communication challenges may require engagement with a family or staff member.

5   My suggestion is to use port wine for four reasons: 1) Traditionally port has been commonly used as Communion wine; 2) Port has a strong taste and some older people have a decreased sense of taste; 3) Port stores well after opening; 4) Port is cheap.

This isn't a theological position, but a practical one as wafers will dissolve on the tongue, whereas bread can be 'doughy'. Additionally, wafers are a more traditional option and provide a visual cue, particularly for people living with dementia. Finally, rice biscuits or cakes are a good gluten-free option.

If you've been counting, you'll have noticed that providing a full range of options for Communion may require up to ten 'elements'.[6] This can be intimidating, and lead to the question: is it too hard?[7] The answer comes from the pivotal disability theologian Hauerwas who states:

> If the word is preached and the sacraments served without the presence of the mentally handicapped, then it may be that we are less than the body of Christ.[8]

I believe we must make the effort to extend this challenge to not simply the 'handicapped',[9] but also to older people and people living with dementia.

With regard to celebrating Communion, it's important to briefly engage with some other practicalities that

---

6   1) Alcoholic wine; 2) alcoholic wine mildly thick; 3) alcoholic wine moderately thick; 4) alcoholic wine very thick; 5) non-alcoholic wine; 6) non-alcoholic wine mildly thick; 7) non-alcoholic wine moderately thick; 8) non-alcoholic wine very thick; 9) wafers; and 10) rice cakes.

7   Please note this array of options is also important when serving food, for example during morning tea after church.

8   'The Church and the Mentally Handicapped: A Continuing Challenge to the Imagination' by Stanley Hauerwas, in *Critical Reflections on Stanley Hauerwas' Theology of Disability, Disabling Society, Enabling Theology,* (ed) John Swinton, (The Haworth Pastoral Press, 2004), p. 60.

9   While the term 'handicapped' is rightly outdated as it's offensive, I've included this quote because Hauerwas' position is profound.

apply specifically to older adults and people living with dementia: mobility, a common cup, intinction (or tincture) and pre-packaged Communion.

In many Communion services, people come to the front to receive the elements. This is a problem for people who live with impaired mobility. The usual solution is to take Communion to them where they're sitting, but this is problematic as it emphasises their lack of mobility and can therefore feel stigmatising. A more inclusive approach is to serve Communion to everyone in the same manner, for example taking Communion to everyone.

Again, traditionally Communion wine was served from a silver[10] chalice with the cup being rotated and wiped between participants. Using a silver chalice can be a great tool to help cue people living with dementia that church and Communion are happening. However, from a hygiene perspective, serving the wine from a chalice is problematic, not to mention that it would require up to eight chalices to accommodate the diversity of 'wines' required.

Nevertheless, a silver chalice can still be useful for intinction. Intinction (or tincture) is the practice of dipping a wafer into the wine before giving it to the congregant. Traditionally, the moistened wafer was placed in their open mouth, but a better option is to place it in their hand. The advantage of intinction is that it can resolve challenges around swallowing as it moistens the wafer and thickens the wine.

---

10 Interestingly, silver was not only used to emphasise the value of Communion, but due to the view that silver provided a level of sterility.

A modern innovation used successfully by some churches is the use of pre-packaged Communion, which consists of a sealed small glass of grape juice and a wafer. This innovation is great in terms of hygiene, but it can be problematic for many older people and people living with dementia because trying to open the plastic seals can be very challenging.

I suspect for many Christians these practicalities will have raised issues. I hope, though, that you will be encouraged and equipped to celebrate Communion effectively not only in care home and dementia contexts but also in all Communion services.

Further resources

Critical Reflections on Stanley Hauerwas' Theology of Disability, Disabling Society, Enabling Theology, John Swinton (ed) (The Haworth Pastoral Press, 2004).

Concluding Remarks

Thank you not only for reading this book, but also for caring enough about older people and people living with dementia to seek to improve how you share Jesus' love with them. To quote from James 1: 'Religion that God our Father accepts as pure and faultless is this: to look after orphans and widows'. Moreover, when we love older people and people living with dementia, we have the magnificent privilege of loving both God and our neighbour.

If this privilege were easy this book would be unnecessary, but it's often challenging on multiple levels. My hope is this book will serve as a reference tool when you're facing those challenges. I also hope some of you may be led to contemplate full-time ministry with older people or people living with dementia.

Irrespective of how and where you serve, please don't forget older people, or people living with dementia.

Appendix

Creating a Sensory Garden

A garden is a wonderful space to engage with or simply to enjoy. Sadly, many people living in care homes are deprived of the opportunity to enjoy a garden. Having created gardens in two multi-storey care homes, I hope this summary will inspire you to consider creating a sensory or other garden and provide you with some basic how-to instructions. I've started with the challenges and solutions, but be encouraged: a sensory garden is eminently achievable.

Challenges and solutions
Safety

We all want our gardens to be safe. However, safety is relative. I've a built a three-storey tree house and my kids love it, but such a feature isn't appropriate for all gardens.

Here are some thoughts about how to keep people safe:

- <u>Potting mix</u>: contains micro-organisms harmful to people. So, keep the mix damp, and wear gloves and a face mask.

- <u>Trip hazards</u>: these are a huge issue in a care home context. The garden should provide appropriate walkways and minimise potential trip hazards (e.g. hoses, tools and plants).

- <u>Ponds/fountains</u>: are a great feature in any garden and particularly in a care home garden, but they need to be designed to minimise the risk of drowning. Options include fencing, limiting depth, and making sure ponds are raised so that if someone was to fall in they cannot become trapped upside down.

- <u>Poisons</u>: are a real danger in the garden. Pesticides and some fertilisers need to be stored in a secure manner. However, the choice of plants is also very significant as many plants are poisonous, and some edible plants have poisonous parts (e.g. tomato/potato leaves and stems; rhubarb leaves). This is a particular issue in care homes where people living with sensory loss or dementia may eat all the parts of a plant. My suggestion is to limit the planting of any poisonous plant and to be very careful about signage[1] that encourages people to eat plants. In a high-risk area I would suggest only planting totally edible plants.

Maintenance

Anyone who is familiar with care homes has seen garden beds and pots either bare, with the remains of plants, or

---

1 Effective signage is a core part of a garden designed for older people and people living with dementia. If the garden is to be multisensory then at least some part of it should be edible.

growing weeds. Indeed, I would suggest the hardest part of a garden in a care home context is maintenance. So, design your garden with maintenance in mind! Work out what level of maintenance it needs to survive and design it accordingly. I recommend:

1. Minimise the need for watering

   - Use large pots and avoid terracotta ones unless they're sealed.[2] Large pots also make access easier for people who struggle to bend or are in a wheelchair.

   - Consider a pond and aquatic plants.

   - Grow plants that don't require frequent watering (e.g. bromeliads, geraniums, succulents and palms).

   - Install a watering system.

   - Use a mulch (e.g. straw or pebbles) and ensure the mulch is too large or too small to become a choking hazard.

   - Consider inorganic components such as statues, wall hangings, wind chimes, fountains and even artificial flowers.[3]

2. Maximise plant longevity

   - Plan for the light and climate. Some plants will struggle in shady positions while others will struggle in full sun.

---

2   If terracotta pots haven't been sealed they lose water quickly.

3   Care should be taken to avoid features that could be associated with idolatry (e.g. statues of gods or goddesses and some wind chimes).

- Plant hardy plants that love your climate.
3. Maximise maintenance
    - Engage the people who will maintain the garden during the design stage. In other words, invite residents, staff, family members and volunteers to be involved.

Resources

Every garden is different and requires different resources to both construct and maintain it. With infinite resources we can grow anything but here are some suggestions if resources are limited.

- Donations: Ask for donations from your community (e.g. staff, residents' family members and local garden clubs). For example, we were exceptionally blessed by the generosity of our local hardware store. They donated plants, posts, a shed, fountains and lots more, and installed a number of these gifts for us.

- Propagation: Consider propagating plants either from seeds or cuttings. This has the added bonus of being a great way to involve care home and local community residents in the garden.

- Be creative/recycle! There are lots of ideas online. A great starting point would be to Google 'reusing a pallet'.

Design suggestions

Great garden design will achieve your garden goals with whatever resources you have available. It also needs to be tailored to your climate. For example, one of the multisensory gardens I designed was on a large balcony with a poor aspect.

Here's a summary of its key features:

Sound

- A fountain.
- Wind chimes.

Sight

- A flower bed.
- A flowage table or shade bed with animal statues 'hidden' and a sign asking people to find the animals.

Smell

- Scented plants (herbs and flowers).

Taste

- A vegetable or herb garden.

Touch

- Succulents, grasses.
- Outdoor gas heaters. (These also made the garden more usable in winter.)
- A chiminea. (Only light it when you can supervise it.)

A greenhouse

- Some of our residents and a staff member are passionate about orchids so we purchased a polycarbonate greenhouse as this was required given the climate.

Bromeliad bed

- Residents wanted to grow bromeliads.

Succulent bed

- Residents wanted to grow succulents.

Fishpond

- A round fishpond on a timber stand[4] with a sign that read 'please count the fish'.

Dwarf citrus in large pots

- Most residents remembered growing citrus. Citrus plants also have pretty perfumed flowers and edible fruit.

Native stingless beehive

- A safe and engaging way to keep bees. They are great for the environment and pollination.

Signs

- As our focus was people living in a nursing home, we used lots of Montessori signage.[5]

I hope this encourages you to build a sensory garden for people who are living in a care home near you.

---

4   The stand made it harder to fall in and elevated the fish for better viewing.

5   For more information please read *Montessori Methods for Dementia: Focusing on the Person and the Prepared Environment*, by Gail Eliot.

Further resources

The Bible Garden, (Australian Centre for Christianity and Culture, 2016).

'The Impact of a Dementia-Friendly Garden Design on People With Dementia in a Residential Aged Care Facility: A Case Study'. Motealleh, P., Moyle, W., Jones, C., and Dupre, K. (2022), *HERD*, *15*(2), 196–218. https://doi.org/10.1177/19375867211063489.

'"My father is a gardener …": A systematic narrative review on access and use of the garden by people living with dementia', Newton, R., Keady, J., Tsekleves, E., and Adams OBE, S. (2021) *Health & Place*, 68. https://doi.org/10.1016/j.healthplace.2021.102516.

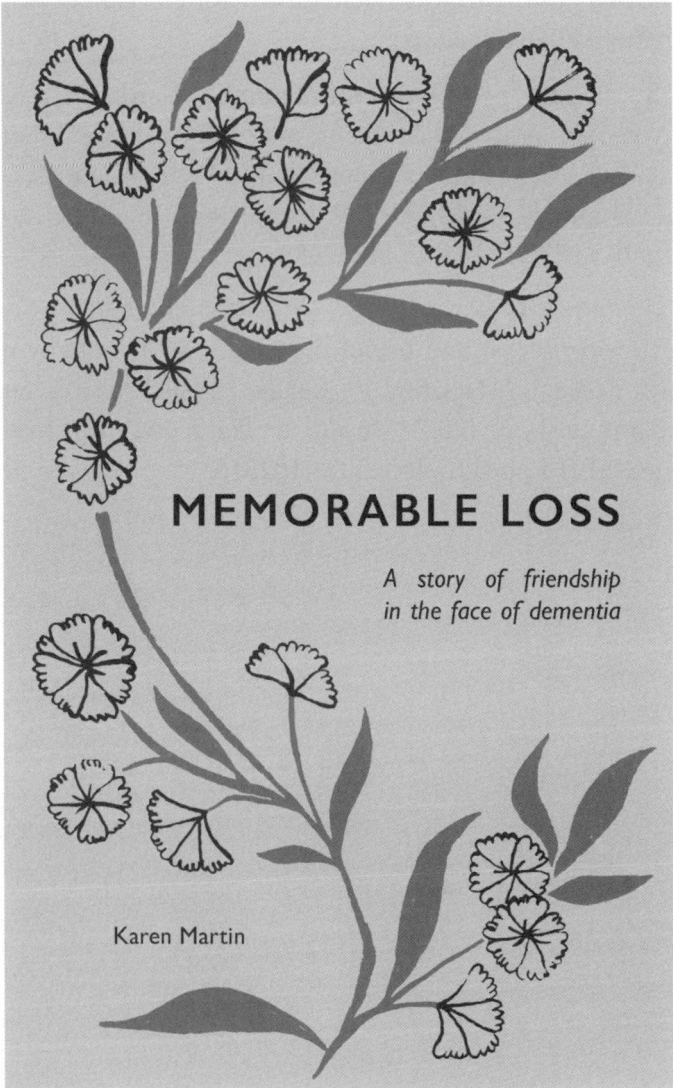

MEMORABLE LOSS

*A story of friendship
in the face of dementia*

Karen Martin

Memorable Loss
by Karen Martin

Dementia is experienced in different forms, in different ways and is coped with differently by different people, but with nearly 10 million new cases every year, it is something many people face. It's tough on those with the disease, but it is also incredibly hard for the loved ones around them.

Karen Martin's story about her friend Kathleen, however, is overwhelmingly one of love and persistence. Despite their nearly half–century age difference, their commonality drew them to each other, and their genuine friendship uplifted them both.

Charting the story from pre–diagnosis to Kathleen's eventual passing, this moving tale highlights the difficulties and joys of facing dementia, through the lens of friendship.

ISBN: 978-1-5271-1002-1

HELPING
the
SUFFERING

*Autobiographical insights
on supporting those in pain*

James & Jennie Muldoon

Helping the Suffering
by James & Jennie Muldoon

Seeing someone you love hurting, and feeling like you can do nothing to help, is hard. We are so nervous about making their suffering worse that we are paralysed into doing nothing.

James and Jennie Muldoon are familiar with suffering. They tell their story here, explain how they were supported and comforted by their brothers and sisters in Christ, and give ideas for where to start when we are helping those in pain.

ISBN: 978-1-5271-0558-4

WHY DO İ SUFFER?
SUFFERING & THE SOVEREIGNTY OF GOD

J O H N   C U R R I D

Why Do I Suffer?
by John Currid

Why does God allow suffering? It's a question that, in one form or another rears its head time and again. Whether it comes from someone who has just lost a loved one, been diagnosed with an incurable illness or even just surveyed the plight of the poor in the third world. A few days after the terrorist attacks of 9/11 the question that was being asked around the world was – Where was God in this? John Currid brings biblical teaching to bear. God does work in suffering, he is not a worried observer unwilling or unable to intervene, rather he has a purpose at work and is in control.

ISBN: 978-1-78191-506-6

Christian Focus Publications

Our mission statement
Staying Faithful

In dependence upon God we seek to impact the world through literature faithful to His infallible Word, the Bible. Our aim is to ensure that the Lord Jesus Christ is presented as the only hope to obtain forgiveness of sin, live a useful life and look forward to heaven with Him.

Our Books are published in four imprints:

◁◯✕ CHRISTIAN FOCUS

Popular works including biographies, commentaries, basic doctrine and Christian living.

◁◯✕ MENTOR

Books written at a level suitable for Bible College and seminary students, pastors, and other serious readers. The imprint includes commentaries, doctrinal studies, examination of current issues and church history.

◁◯✕ CHRISTIAN HERITAGE

Books representing some of the best material from the rich heritage of the church.

◁◯✕ CF4KIDS

Children's books for quality Bible teaching and for all age groups: Sunday school curriculum, puzzle and activity books; personal and family devotional titles, biographies and inspirational stories – because you are never too young to know Jesus!

Christian Focus Publications Ltd,
Geanies House, Fearn, Ross-shire,
IV20 1TW, Scotland, United Kingdom.
www.christianfocus.com